Decoupage
YOUR Home

Decoupage
YOUR
Home

Fransie Snyman

SEARCH PRESS

ACKNOWLEDGEMENTS

Thank you very much to Basil Lentner of Heritage Craft Products who supplied the products for the projects. Your products are excellent and made the completion of the projects pure pleasure. Thank you to my sisters, Retha and Wilsia, who assisted with the projects. Without your help I would not have been able to manage everything. A huge, big thank you to my husband, Paul, who did all the 'hard' work – painting, hammering, sanding and waxing. It made my job so much easier! Thanks to Kenny, the photographer, for the calm and professional manner in which you always handle the shoots. Last but not least, thanks to Liezl who once again did a brilliant layout and made the projects look so beautiful in the book.

First published in Great Britain in 2017
Search Press Limited
Wellwood, North Farm Road,
Tunbridge Wells, Kent TN2 3DR

Originally published in 2017 by Metz Press
1 Cameronians Avenue, Welgemoed 7530, South Africa

Copyright © Metz Press 2017
Copyright text © Fransie Snyman
Photography copyright © Metz Press

Suppliers

Although every attempt has been made to ensure that all the materials and equipment used in this book are currently available, the Publishers cannot guarantee that this will always be the case. If you have difficulty in obtaining any of the items mentioned, then suitable alternatives should be used instead.

For details of suppliers, please visit the Search Press website: www.searchpress.com

ISBN 13: 978-1-78221-576-9

Publisher	Wilsia Metz
Photographer	Kenneth Irvine, Fancy Shmancy
Designer	Liezl Maree
Proofreader	Nikki Metz
Reproduction	Robert Wong, Color Fuzion

Printed and bound by
1010 Printing International Ltd, China

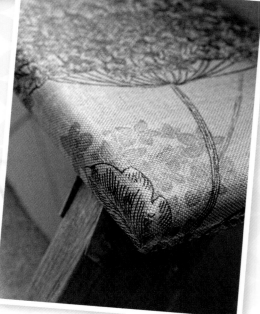

Contents

Introduction

The word *decoupage* comes from the French word *découper* which means to cut. Decoupage is a craft technique that has been used since the 12th Century to decorate the surface of uninteresting pieces of furniture by cutting out paper images, gluing it to the furniture and applying several layers of varnish. It was a relatively easy way to decorate furniture, even though it was time consuming because of the many layers of varnish that had to be applied over the images and the sanding of the varnish so that the images would look like part of the surface.

Decoupage is one of those age-old art forms that keeps on surfacing and is practised in different forms. In the crafting community, the traditional technique is no longer necessarily applied. Crafters tend to call anything that can be pasted and covered, decoupage. It no longer needs to be paper images that have been cut out – articles to be decoupaged can also be covered in paper, fabric or lace.

A large portion of the book is dedicated to objects that have been restored. Decrepit, old pieces of furniture, suitcases, storage tins and more, were given a new lease of life by applying paint techniques and decoupage. I am sure there are people who still stick to the traditional way of doing decoupage, but the projects in this book were all done very quickly. You still need a little patience in order to achieve a neat, smooth finish, but having to spend weeks applying layer upon layer of varnish, is not applicable in this case.

Because the basic techniques are virtually the same in all the projects, I discuss the techniques before describing each project separately. If you are an expert decoupeur, you might want to skip this section, but it is available for reference. If you want to try your hand at decoupage for the first time, it is important to read the introduction carefully before you begin.

The projects in the book are meant to serve as examples and inspiration for you to undertake your own projects. If you use bases that are different to the ones I use, then you will find that you cannot precisely follow all the steps of each project, but you will get an indication of what to do with your bases.

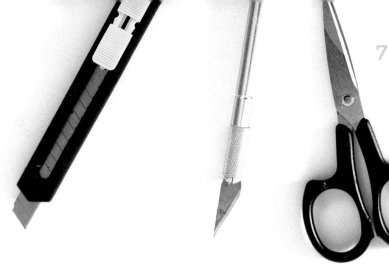

What you need

Tools and equipment

There are certain tools you absolutely must have. Most of these are readily available at craft shops or hardware stores. Buy good quality, durable tools which will produce the best results for your projects.

CRAFT KNIFE

You need a good craft knife in order to do detailed cutting neatly and precisely. Make sure that the blade of the knife is always sharp otherwise it will spoil your cutting by tearing the paper. Always use a craft knife with a sharp point so that you can easily cut into tiny corners.

PAIR OF SCISSORS

A small, sharp pair of good quality scissors is essential for cutting out pictures you use for decoupage. The scissors must also have a sharp point so that you can cut into tiny corners. I have found that a pair of nail scissors or embroidery scissors works very well. Always put your decoupage scissors away after using them (hide them from your husband and children) and only use them for decoupage.

STEEL RULER

Because you will use a sharp knife for cutting, it is advisable to also use a steel ruler. If you use a plastic ruler, you can easily damage it with your knife. Be careful not to cut into the sides of the steel ruler, as this will result in a blunt blade.

CUTTING MAT

It is worth investing in a good cutting mat. It is best to buy one that is self healing. It heals itself after you have cut on it, so the surface is always smooth. If you keep the cutting mat nice and clean and you do not spill glue or podge on it, it can be used for many years.

TEFLON CRAFT MAT

This craft mat consists of a thin layer of Teflon. It protects your work surface against stains, glue and heat and nothing sticks to it. I don't know how I ever managed without one! If you spill any glue or paint on it, it can be removed quickly and easily by using the side of a ruler or palette knife to scratch it off.

BRAYERS

A brayer or small rubber roller is handy when podging big pictures, whole sheets of paper or fabric. I recently discovered small silicon rollers that work very well on polymer clay. The silicon roller works well because podge and glue do not stick to it and it can be cleaned easily.

BRUSHES AND APPLICATORS

It is very important to work with good quality brushes and applicators. This ensures that your projects will always be of the highest quality. Few things are more frustrating than paintbrush bristles coming loose and ending up in the glue or paint. Sometimes it is necessary to use a small sponge roller to apply the paint in order to achieve a smooth, even finish. You can also use a flat sponge applicator. These sponge applicators come in different widths so you are able to choose the right size for the specific task at hand.

When working with napkins, it is important to use a soft, good quality brush. The quality of your brush will determine the success of your project.

Because the projects are covered in so many layers of podge, you can keep your brushes and sponge applicators in a plastic bag to prevent them from drying out between layers. You can then use the same brush for the following layers, and at the end of the day you can wash all your brushes and sponge applicators in soapy water and dry them thoroughly.

Do not use the same brushes for paint and podge. Pigment often remains behind in your paint brushes, irrespective of how well you wash them, and this can leave unwelcome colour on your project if you use the same brush for podge.

WET WIPES

It is essential to have wet wipes on hand when working with glue and podge. They are used to wipe excess glue and podge from your project and your hands and to clean your roller. It is virtually impossible to work with paper if your hands are full of glue; I find wet wipes particularly handy when I use my fingers to remove a bit of glue or podge from a surface.

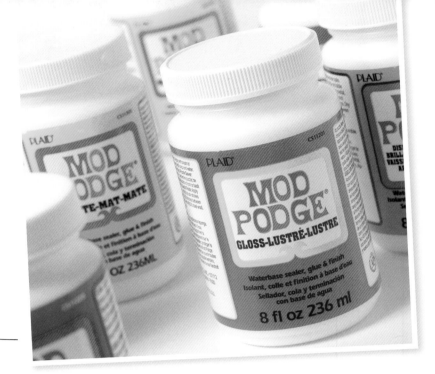

Products

PODGE

The most important product needed for decoupage, is obviously podge. Podge serves two purposes – it is used as glue and it is used to protect the base you work on as well as the embellishment. Sometimes it is better to first use glue to stick down pictures, especially if you are working with a very smooth surface or if the pictures consist of a thick material such as vinyl. There is a large variety of podge available made to suit specific projects.

Some websites provide recipes to make your own podge. I have found, however, that it is best to buy products manufactured for a specific purpose. Because I want my projects to be long lasting and durable, I have opted to buy the real thing rather than make my own podge.

Every crafter has his or her favourite brand, so use what you like and what works for you. If you feel that your secret recipe works for you, then go ahead and make your own podge. I find that the Heritage range of products works best for me and there is a large variety available. These products are distributed in the UK under the label First Choice Crafts. In the US the Mod Podge range can be used.

Ordinary podge comes in three different types of finish – satin, matt and gloss.

I mostly used satin podge because it produces a really luxurious satin finish. I usually apply three to four layers of podge, wait for the podge to dry and then sand it with 1000-grit sandpaper. I then apply four more layers of podge. I have learnt from experience that this podge does not work well as an adhesive. If a project requires using an adhesive, it is better to use wood glue that dries clear.

Matt podge has no shine to it and I mostly use it on pieces of furniture where only the paint and pictures need protection.

Gloss podge has a nice shine to it, but it is not too shiny. If you want a product to be really shiny, use a gloss varnish.

Heritage also has a range of podges available for specific types of decoupage.

The specific products are:

Napkin Podge

This is used when you work with napkins (serviettes). Because this podge is not as sticky as other types of podge, the napkins do not easily tear.

Candle Podge

This is used to decoupage candles. This podge does not give off smoke when the candle is burning. If you do no have access to candle medium, adhere the images by using heat from a hair dryer.

Outdoor Podge

This product is recommended for outdoor items such as veranda tables, pot plants, etcetera.

Glitter Podge

This contains glitter powder that makes the object shimmer when it catches the light. This podge has a rough finish because of the glitter powder.

CPG Podge

This is recommended when working on glass and ceramics. Items are covered in this podge and baked in an oven. This seals the podge completely making it possible to wash the item in warm, soapy water.

ADHESIVE

Wood glue

Sometimes it is better to use wood glue rather than podge to paste pictures. I used glue rather than podge to paste all the photos for the photograph wall. If you apply very thin, even layers of glue, you will have fewer air bubbles than when applying podge. The biggest drawback when using glue rather than podge, is that the glue dries quicker than the podge, so you have to work very accurately and quickly when positioning.

Spray adhesive

I used spray adhesive to glue the napkins onto paper for the kiddies' table on page 110. It results in sturdier images, making them easier to podge.

VARNISH

Although varnish is often used to add a finishing touch to an object, it is really only necessary if the object is going to be handled a lot or if people are going to sit on it. Use any brand available to you.

Decu Varnish

This varnish is suitable to seal porous surfaces such as plaster or terracotta and is available in a gloss or matt finish.

Seal Skin

This varnish dries very quickly and also gives projects a high gloss finish.

Heavy Duty Varnish/ Polyurethane hard varnish

This is also available in a gloss or matt finish and is recommended for outdoor items. I used it on the kitchen stools on page 54 because the stools can easily be scratched or damaged during everyday use.

Candle Varnish

This product is used to give candles a smooth, shiny finish. Coloured varnish is also available and can be used to change the colour of the candle. This varnish does not affect how the candle burns and is merely applied to change the appearance of the candle.

Liquid Glass

This is a product that can be used to achieve a very durable, high gloss finish that looks like glass. You could also use ICE Resin® or Pratliglo®.

PAINT

Chalk paint

The arrival of chalk paint changed the way in which objects are prepared prior to painting. I use this paint a lot because it reduces the amount of time and energy needed for preparation before decoupage. Because chalk paint clings to any surface, your object does not need priming before applying the final colour. Chalk paint is available in a variety of beautiful colours. I used various brands because each brand manufactures its own colours and this gives you a much bigger variety to choose from.

Although chalk paint is usually sealed with wax, I often used podge instead of wax, as mentioned in specific projects.

Acrylic paint

Heritage acrylic paint is a water-based product containing a high quality dye.

It shows no separation if left standing for a lengthy period and can be applied to any surface. It provides excellent protection and you seldom need to apply more than one coat. It also comes

in a variety of colours and it is easy to mix colours if you cannot find the exact colour that you are looking for. Remember – less is more! Add small bits of a darker colour to a light colour, mix thoroughly and test the colour before adding more dark paint.

Use any acrylic paint but always keep durability in mind.

Spray paint

I discovered that spray paint works particularly well on plastic and provides excellent protection. It made for an excellent finish to the toy box (see page 102) which was spray painted before I decoupaged it with fabric.

Tins often have coloured motifs, rust spots or other stains that remain visible if you use thin paper or napkins to cover them. This is when white spray paint comes in handy. I spray painted all the tins for my projects white before découpaging them.

SANDPAPER

Sandpaper is available in different grades of coarseness. The higher the number printed on the back of the sandpaper, the finer the sandpaper. Sandpaper with a coarser grit (lower number) is used to sand wood and a finer grit (higher number) is used to sand over podge. I always make sure that I have at least four grades of sandpaper at hand.

What can you decoupage?

"If it stands still for longer than 20 seconds, you can decoupage it!" The possibilities are endless. If you are enthusiastic about the art form, the execution thereof is limitless. Virtually any surface can be decoupaged if prepared properly.

WOOD

Raw wood and compressed wood (MDF) can be decoupaged with equal success. Wooden blanks in various shapes and sizes are available at most craft and hardware stores and are mostly used for découpaging. The same wooden blanks are used for mosaic and other craft forms, so they are readily available. If you use raw wood, it may be necessary to sand the wood before you work with images and podge because the sections you will decoupage must not be too rough.

GLASS

You can decoupage on any glass and if it is covered in CPG podge and baked in the oven, it becomes heat resistant and can be washed. I do not recommend washing it in a dishwasher. To be safe, rather wash by hand in a basin filled with soapy water.

Glass windows can be decoupaged with lace to make them less transparent or to merely decorate them. It can, therefore, be functional or decorative.

METAL

A large variety of galvanised steel products such as watering-cans, buckets, flower-boxes, pans, etcetera, are available. With the arrival of chalk paint, the steel does not even need priming before it is decoupaged. The chalk paint clings to any surface and you just need to wait patiently for it to dry completely before applying the podge.

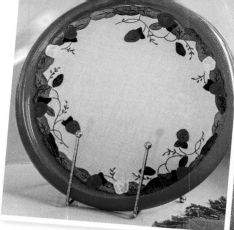

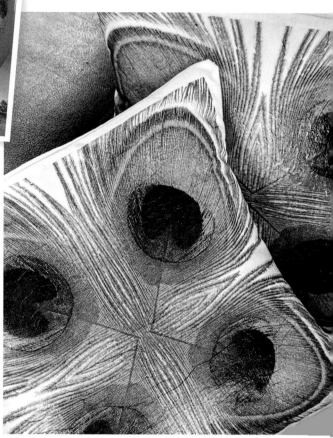

PLASTIC

In the age of plastic, you can jazz up any old plastic objects that no longer look good by découpaging them. Most of us (of a certain age) probably have a round plastic tray that no longer looks good and in most houses where there are children, you will find a plastic children's table. These items can be revamped by découpaging them.

Recycling and reusing are the right thing to do and this is where the decoupage-technique comes in handy.

WALLS AND FLOORS

Even walls and floors can be decoupaged. A durable, hard varnish must be used to finish off decoupaged floors. A good paper to use when découpaging walls, is scrapbook paper. You often buy more paper than you need. A bedroom wall can be made to look very interesting if you decoupage it with paper blocks of 30 cm x 30 cm, giving it a tiled look.

CERAMICS

You can decoupage on unglazed or glazed ceramics. If you decoupage on glazed ceramics, you can prevent images from peeling by applying CPG podge and baking the ceramics in the oven. If you have leftover tiles, you should consider podging a pretty picture or piece of fabric onto the tile, finishing it off with CPG podge and baking it in the oven to make it water resistant. It can then be used as a pot stand or as a decorative element in the home.

FABRIC OR TEXTILES

You can make a beautiful cushion by découpaging a pretty napkin onto fabric and using the fabric to make a cushion cover. You can jazz up a simple rag-bag by découpaging it. Some chain stores sell bags in all kinds of plain colours. These bags become lovely gifts once they have been decoupaged. Tablecloths and placemats can also be successfully decoupaged.

LEATHER

If you want to give someone a pretty diary with a leather cover as a gift, you can personalise it by, for example, découpaging it with a pretty photograph. It is important to apply podge to the entire cover to prevent the photograph from coming loose.

What can you use for decoupage?

Paper is traditionally used for decoupage but, thanks to the development of so many special products, fabric, ribbon, vinyl and napkins can also be used. When working with three-dimensional objects such as a tray with a glass inset, you can even use unconventional items such as coffee beans.

PAPER

Your choice of paper is virtually unlimited because there is such a large variety of paper and pictures available for decoupage.

Most craft shops sell paper that is specially manufactured with decoupage in mind. This paper generally has a variety of smaller pictures that can be used together or individually. Every sheet of paper that I bought, could be used for more than one project.

Wrapping paper is slightly thinner than decoupage paper, but is also suitable to use. Once you start découpaging, you will view gift wrap, often torn from a gift and discarded, in a completely different light!

Scrapbook paper is available at most craft shops and is a limitless source of pictures that can be used for decoupage. This paper is usually slightly thicker and firmer than gift wrap and works particularly well on objects that are slightly damaged. Because the paper is fairly thick, it easily conceals the damaged areas and you need not spend too much time sanding the object or using wood filler to make it smooth.

MAGAZINES AND NEWSPAPERS

Magazines and newspapers are made of very thin paper and the possibility exists that the reverse side of the paper or picture that you are using, will shine through when podge is applied to it. If the paper is too thin but you really want to use a specific picture or photograph, make a colour copy of it and use that instead. Just make sure that the copy is made with a laser printer or copying machine.

DECOPATCH PAPER

Decopatch paper is very thin (20gsm) but very robust. It is manufactured with a special UV coating and finish, making it easy to use in corners and on curves without it tearing. It comes in beautiful colours and designs so you do not have to do any cutting. When torn, no small fragments remain on the edges. Because the colours are so bright and the designs so interesting, it can be used to make various collages. It is available online and from a number of craft shops.

PHOTOGRAPHS

It would be wonderful to create a personal gift by découpaging original photographs but you cannot do this because the podge would react with the coating on the photograph. You can, however, make a copy of the photograph and use that. The photographs on the photo wall on page 42 were printed in colour on coated paper. The copies are very clear and easy to work with. Once again, make sure that the copies were made with a laser printer or copying machine. You do not have to use photographs of people only. You can also use scenic or wildlife photographs (see the tin below).

COMPUTER PICTURES

If you want to use pictures that are on your computer, make sure that you use a laser printer. If an inkjet printer is used, the ink in the pictures will run the moment it comes into contact with the podge. Make sure that pictures downloaded from the Internet are not copyrighted or that you can pay to download them – especially if you intend selling your products.

TRANSFERS AND VINYL PICTURES

Strictly speaking, the use of vinyl pictures and words as well as photo transfers is not decoupage, but it can make life a lot easier for you. You can make your own photo transfers by using Heritage Transfer Glaze. The technique is discussed in detail on page 27.

CARDS

The pictures on used greeting cards or new ones can also be used for decoupage. I like to keep all the cards I receive – if you have a supply of these, go through them and see which pictures you can possibly use. This will work particularly well with items that have sentimental value and which you associate with specific occasions or people.

STAMPS

If you, or a family member, are an avid stamp collector then you probably have a supply of used stamps that are pretty but not necessarily valuable. These stamps can be used for decoupage. In my previous book, *Frames Galore* (Metz Press 2016), there's a beautiful example of a frame that was decoupaged with stamps.

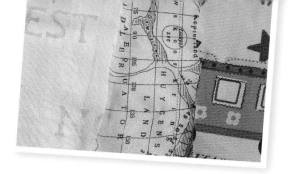

WASHI TAPE

Washi tape is colourful, robust masking tape. It originated in Japan but nowadays it is manufactured all over the world. It is made from the bark fibre of a specific tree and is totally bio-degradable. It is easy to use because it is not too sticky at first and can easily be removed if you accidentally position it incorrectly. Once you are satisfied with how you have positioned it, give it a firm rub and then seal it with podge. It is handy to add finishing touches to pictures or photographs in a collage.

NAPKINS

Napkins are generally used in decoupage because they are nice and thin and do not have to be covered in layers and layers of varnish. The variety of napkins that are available and suitable for decoupage, is absolutely astounding. Many craft shops sell packs of two to four napkins especially for decoupage. It is very handy to be able to buy napkins in these quantities rather than having to buy an entire pack of napkins of which only a few may be used. While writing this book, I could not resist buying every pretty pack of napkins that I came across. I probably have enough napkins to last me the next 10 years!

When using napkins for decoupage, make sure that they are of a very good quality. Napkins tear easily and napkins of a poor quality tear even more easily, making them very difficult to work with.

Use a soft brush of a very good quality when working with napkins. Not only does this make the process easier, it also guarantees a professional finish.

TEXTILES

You can use any type of fabric, netting or ribbon for decoupage. When buying fabric for a project, make sure that you take enough to complete the project. It will be a rather disappointing not to be able to complete your project because you cannot obtain more of the same fabric!

The thicker the fabric, the more podge you will need because thicker fabric absorbs more podge. Thinner fabric is easier to use and will require less podge. You can also cut motifs out of the fabric for use. In this case, cover the motif in a layer of podge and allow it to dry before you cut it out, to prevent fraying.

If you work with lace, it is advisable to use a stencil brush and soak the lace in podge to ensure that it clings firmly and does not come loose.

VINYL

Vinyl table cloths are often brightly coloured with pretty designs that you can cut out for decoupage. Vinyl is easy to use because it does not fray when you cut it and it does not tear. Vinyl motifs should not be used on objects that are handled a lot. Because the vinyl is thicker than paper, it will stand out from a surface onto which it has been podged more than paper and can easily hook on something and be pulled off.

Techniques

The basic technique in decoupage is very simple. You cut and podge. You can cut out pictures or use big sheets of paper or fabric that cover the entire object. Several techniques are applicable to more than one project in the book and rather than repeating them at each project, I discuss them here with cross references at the specific projects.

Preparation of bases

When you decoupage, the correct preparation of the base is very important to ensure that the finished project is what you envisaged. It might not be the most exciting part of the project, but it must not be neglected.

Your preparation will be largely determined by the condition of the object that you will decoupage as well as the material it is made of.

Raw wood must first be sanded to remove splinters from the surface of the wood.

If you are going to use old pieces of furniture covered in varnish, it is imperative that you first sand off all the varnish to ensure that anything you paint or podge onto it does not peel. If the surface is very rough, you can apply gesso paste or wood filler and sand it before you paint or podge.

The cement pots on page 114 had a very rough finish, so jointing plaster was used to make them smooth before being painted and decoupaged.

If you are going to decoupage galvanised objects and not use chalk paint, a base coat must be applied to the item. Plascon Galvogrip Metal Primer is available at any hardware store and can be used for this purpose.

Sometimes it is only necessary to wipe the object with a damp cloth to make sure that it is clean before you paint or podge.

Cutting

Cutting is an important part of decoupage and you will often find that cutting out a number of pictures for a project, is the most time-consuming part. When using a pair of scissors to cut out pictures and motifs, it is always better to move the paper held in the hand that is not holding the pair of scissors and for the other hand to control the blades. It is easier if you rest your arm on a table.

If you do not feel like cutting out, do it while watching television. Time passes quickly and before you know it, you will have cut out a whole lot of pictures.

Store excess pictures in a filing sleeve in a ring binder.

Any pictures on ordinary paper that you want to cut out can first be sealed with a layer of podge, making them easier to cut out with a small pair of scissors. You cannot do this with napkins.

Whether you cut motifs out of paper or napkins, it is advisable to use a craft knife to cut out finer details. Once this is done, use a small pair of scissors to cut along the outside edges of the picture.

When using napkins, it is best to keep all layers together for the cutting out part. You can separate the layers once you have cut out the motifs.

If you are working with a flat object such as a placemat on which paper is podged from side to side, allow the first layer of podge to dry and then use a craft knife to remove the paper from the bottom of the mat.

You can tear pieces of paper instead of cutting. You can either casually tear pieces into different sizes or you can use a paper tearing ruler.

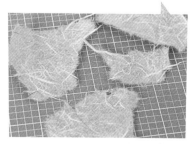

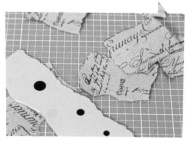

Paint techniques

Various paint techniques work very well with decoupage. Any paint work and paint techniques are usually completed before you begin with the decoupage.

CHALK PAINT

Chalk paint is handy to use because it clings to any surface. If the item you wish to decoupage needs no other preparation, then chalk paint is a good background on which to decoupage. Once you have decoupaged any pictures on the chalk paint surface, apply podge to the entire background to prevent the paint from being scratched off easily.

DRY BRUSH

This technique was used to decorate the nursery organiser on page 104. Apply two coats of acrylic paint to the item and allow to dry thoroughly. Lightly dip a brush in paint of a contrasting colour and paint on a piece of wood offcut or on paper, so that as little paint as possible remains on the brush. Use the almost dry brush to paint over the base colour.

COLOUR WASH

Colour wash looks lovely on raw wood. The colour is very subtle and the wood easily absorbs the paint. It is very easy to master this technique. First you wet the wood with water and then apply very little paint that has also been diluted.

The amount of water you use will be determined by the type of paint. Acrylic paint requires less water than when working with chalk paint. It is best to start with very little paint and lots of water. If you do not achieve the desired effect, repeat the process. You do not need to wait for the paint to dry before applying a little more. If you are not sure what it is going to look like once the paint has dried, wait until it is completely dry before deciding whether you are going to apply another coat of paint or whether you are going to use more water. If you feel that the colour is too intense, add water to the paint until you achieve the desired effect.

Because the wood gets very wet during the colour wash process, make sure that it is completely dry before you begin pasting or podging.

DISTRESSING

It is very popular nowadays to paint objects and then sand them to create a distressed look. You can use various methods to achieve this effect.

Paint and sand

This technique requires the application of a single coat of paint to the object and when the paint is completely dry, it is sanded here and there – usually only on the edges of the object. Use 600-grit sandpaper. This technique was used on the headboard on page 82.

You can use paint in two different colours to add depth to the distressed look. Apply one colour and allow to dry thoroughly. Apply a second coat of paint, usually in a contrasting colour. Make sure the paint is completely dry before sanding the edges and the middle using 600-grit sandpaper.

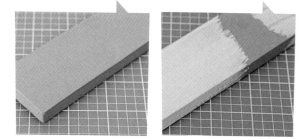

The base colour will become visible here and there and if you sand a little more in certain spots, the wood will also become visible.

Paint and wax/polish

The distressed look on the jewellery box on page 89 was achieved using two contrasting paint colours applied over each other, and wax or floor polish. Paint the item in one colour and allow to dry thoroughly. Apply a second colour over the first coat, followed by a layer of wax or polish once the paint is touch dry. Allow the wax to dry a little before polishing it with a soft cloth. Rub until a little of the top layer comes away and the first coat is revealed. If you are satisfied with the appearance, apply more wax and leave to dry thoroughly – at least five hours. Polish the item until it is smooth and slightly shiny.

Paint and petroleum jelly

When using sandpaper on chalk paint, the sandpaper quickly becomes unusable because the paint forms a thick layer on the sandpaper. If you work with chalk paint, it is advisable to use petroleum jelly to achieve a distressed look. With this technique you also use paint in two different colours.

Apply the first colour and allow the paint to dry thoroughly. Apply the petroleum jelly to the edges of the object and wherever else you want the first coat to be visible.

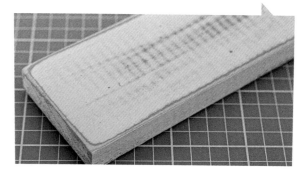

Apply a second coat of paint in a contrasting colour to the entire object. This coat can be slightly thinner than the first.

Once the paint has dried completely, use a

palette knife to scratch away the top layer of paint where the petroleum jelly was applied. The parts covered in petroleum jelly do not dry, so the paint comes off easily.

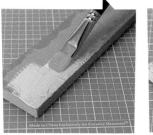

CRACKED-PAINT FINISH

This finish must not be confused with crackle varnish. With the cracked-paint technique, the cracked effect is achieved between two coats of paint, not over a painted surface. The best effect is achieved when you use two contrasting paint colours, preferably with a light colour first and a darker colour applied over it, otherwise the effect is lost completely. It might look like a difficult technique to master, but if you follow the instructions carefully, it is really quite easy.

Apply two to three coats of acrylic paint (preferably a light colour) to the object and leave it to dry completely. Use a sponge applicator to apply a coat of Kwick Crack to the parts that must crack. Try to apply it as evenly as possible.

Allow the Kwick Crack to dry thoroughly. If you are impatient and you apply the next coat too soon, you will not achieve the desired effect.

Once the Kwick Crack is completely dry, apply a coat of acrylic paint in a darker colour. Use even strokes and brush from side to side over the entire surface.

The paint will begin to crack within an hour or two and the light colour will be revealed.

This technique must be completed before you decoupage.

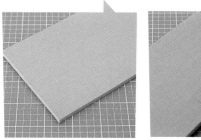

Arrange and podge

PICTURE CUT-OUTS OR MOTIFS

When you plan to podge several pictures onto an object, start by arranging the pictures until you are satisfied with the layout and then podge. You can use a pencil to lightly mark the spot where each picture must be placed or, if possible, leave the pictures in position and podge them one by one.

Apply podge to where you want to paste the pictures on the object and then carefully press the picture down onto the podge. Use your fingers or a small roller to smooth out any air bubbles. Do not get upset if some air bubbles remain. They usually disappear once the podge is dry.

Repeat the process with all the pictures to be podged. If you want to use crackle varnish (see page 25), apply it now. Allow to dry thoroughly and apply four more layers of podge, each in a different direction to the previous layer. Allow each layer to dry before applying the next.

COMPLETE COVERING

If you are covering an object completely in whole sheets of paper or fabric, first apply podge to the entire area to be covered and then carefully place the paper or fabric on the surface. Smooth out any air bubbles using your fingers or a small roller.

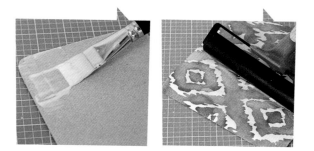

If applicable, use a craft knife or scissors to cut the paper or fabric to size. Apply podge to the entire surface, changing the direction in which it is applied after each layer. Apply one layer from top to bottom and the next from left to right.

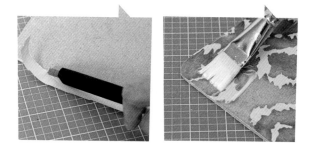

COLLAGE

The paper that is used for decoupage is not necessarily always a picture. Patterned paper can also be cut into regular or irregular shapes and then arranged in a collage on an object. The pieces can be cut or torn in the same size or different

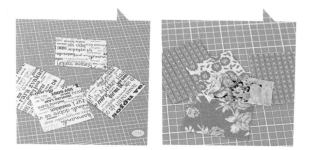

sizes. Make sure that the different pieces do not overlap too much because that will give the object and uneven finish.

Finishes

DISTRESSING PAPER

Once you have pasted paper onto an item, it can be given a distressed look by sanding the paper on the edges and corners of the item. Do the sanding before applying any podge to the paper.

CRACKLE VARNISH

Use Antique Crackle to achieve an antique crackle effect. You apply it once you have applied all the layers of podge to your decoupage work. The product consists of two different fluids that react to each other, thus creating the crackled effect. The base coat is applied first and left to dry thoroughly. Two types of base coats are available – one produces fine cracks and the other bigger cracks. Once the base coat has dried completely, the topcoat is applied. It takes at least five hours or longer for the cracks to form. Be patient and do not presume too quickly that the product is not working.

If you are satisfied that the topcoat is completely dry, use a soft cloth to rub coloured wax, gold-coloured oil paint or any other dark oil paint or ordinary shoe polish into the cracks to emphasise them. Do not rub any water-based paint over the cracks because it will dissolve the topcoat and ruin the effect.

Polish the surface once you have rubbed the wax or polish into the cracks.

RESIN

A high gloss polymer coating, essentially resin, is often applied to the entire surface of a decoupage project to finish it off nicely. Heritage Liquid Glass consists of two liquids that are combined, mixed thoroughly and then poured over a flat surface. There are also other brands and they all have basically the same chemical reaction and appearance. The mixture flows right up to the edges of the surface until it is evenly distributed.

If you see bubbles form, lightly blow on them through a straw to remove. When you are satisfied with the distribution and smooth surface of the liquid, cover the object with a container that is big enough to fit over it loosely and leave it in a dust-free area where nobody will fiddle with it, for at least 24 hours. The longer you leave it to cure, the less chance there is of marks being left by something placed on it.

This finish looks lovely if left to cure properly. It looks like glass and is a durable, hard finish that is suitable for trays.

It is important that the ratio of the two liquids is absolutely equal, otherwise it will not harden. Follow the instructions on the product carefully and preferably work in a dust-free area so that the project is not spoilt by dust that lands on it.

Decoupage under glas

With this technique the usual steps are followed in the reverse order. The motif or paper is decoupaged to the underside of the glass, followed by the application of paint and varnish. Glass plates or shallow glass dishes are more suitable for this technique than deep dishes. If the glass plate is finished with CTP podge and baked in the oven, it can be washed in warm soapy water. It is probably best to use these plates to serve dry items only and to simply clean them with a damp cloth after use.

DECOUPAGE UNDER GLASS WITH A NAPKIN

Work on the back of a glass plate and find the centre. Also find the centre of the napkin and place it face down on the back of the plate. Start at the centre and use a soft brush to apply podge to the napkin. Carefully work from the inside to the outside so that you do not tear the napkin.

Allow the podge to dry completely and apply two to three layers of acrylic paint to the back of the entire plate. Allow to dry completely between layers.

Lift the plate and hold it up to the light to make sure that the paint has been evenly applied. Apply three layers of CPG podge (allow the podge to dry completely between layers) and bake in a 90° C oven for one hour.

If you use a picture or motif from a napkin, use podge to paste the cut out pictures or motifs onto the plate (face down on the back of the plate). Finish with paint and podge in the same way as a plate that is completely covered in a napkin.

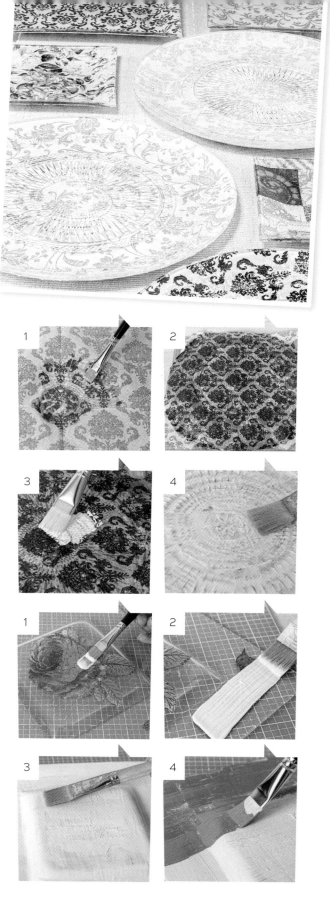

Transfers

Transfer glaze is used to make your own transfers. It is not only used with pictures but also with any pattern paper that is used on rounded surfaces. I used transfer glaze to decorate the drawer knobs of the chest of drawers on page 92. It works very well on curves and this technique will be very handy if you want to decoupage ostrich eggs.

Apply at least six coats of transfer glaze in different directions (from left to right and from top to bottom) to the picture. Allow the glaze to dry after each coat. When the picture is completely dry after applying the last coat, soak it in water for 30 minutes.

Keep the paper completely wet and rub carefully until all the paper has been removed. The result is a thin, pliable motif that looks like plastic.

You can now transfer the motif to the object to be decoupaged. While it is wet, it is slightly sticky, so glue is not needed to fix it in place. Rub the motif onto the surface, making sure that it is even, and cover in a layer of ordinary podge.

This technique is not suitable for pictures that need to be finely cut – they can easily tear during the rubbing process.

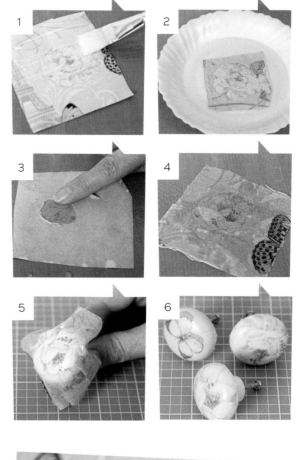

Projects

Travel trunk table

Before

If this travel trunk could speak, it would be fascinating to learn about its wanderings. It was destined for the junk shop when my daughter suggested restoring it and turning it into a coffee table. Choosing the fabric was easy, but the trunk was in a really poor condition and I did not have the time to do all the additional work the project required. My husband, Paul, came to the rescue; he restored the trunk completely and decoupaged it.

1. Remove all the locks, hinges, buckles and wooden strips from the trunk and pull off stickers and labels.

2. Clean the trunk thoroughly to get rid of loose bits of paper and dust.

3. Cut a piece of fabric to size to cover the inside and outside of the lid.

4. Start at the front of the lid and podge fabric onto it. Use a brayer to smooth out any air bubbles. Make neat folds at the corners and use enough podge to push the fabric firmly in place. Take the fabric all the way around and to the inside of the lid, covering it, and leave to dry.

5. Apply four layers of podge in different directions (from top to bottom and from left to right) over the fabric. Allow every layer to dry completely before applying the next.

6. Repeat steps 3–5 on the rest of the trunk – inside and outside.

7. Soak the metal parts in an acid solution for a few minutes to get rid of the rust. Rinse thoroughly and sand lightly with steel wool to remove any remaining rust before spraying it with the gold spray paint.

8. Sand the wooden strips with sandpaper, apply the brown acrylic paint and nail the strips to the suitcase. If you cannot use the original nails, buy new ones.

9. Replace the hinges and clasps and attach the feet to the bottom of the trunk (follow the manufacturer's instructions).

You'll need

Suitcase

Screwdriver

Damp cloth

Fabric to cover the trunk's inside and outside (about 4 m/4²/₅ yd., width 115 cm/45¼ in.)

Pair of scissors

Brushes

Small brayer

Podge – gloss

Acid to remove rust from buckles and clasps

Feet

Steel wool

220-grit sandpaper

Spray paint (matt gold)

Acrylic paint (Heritage: Chocolate)

Coffee table on castors

Before

A coffee table on castors is handy in any room. This small cabinet came from an office where it was used as a printer table. It was on its way to the recycling bin because its hinges were loose and one of the doors was broken, but a friend of mine rescued it and brought it to me to restore. The condition of your cabinet will determine what you need to restore it.

You'll need

Cabinet

Hinges

Screwdriver

Chalk paint (O'Grady's: Grey Violet)

Brushes

Podge – matt

Fabric to decoupage the top of the cabinet

Small brayer

Pair of scissors

1. Repair the cabinet door by replacing the hinges and screwing them down.

2. Give the cabinet a good scrub to get rid of any dirty marks. Apply two coats of chalk paint; make sure that the first is dry before applying the second.

3. Cut the fabric to size to cover the top of the cabinet and fold over the edges.

4. Cover the top of the cabinet in podge and press the fabric onto it. Use the brayer to remove any air bubbles.

5. Podge the fabric over the edges, neatly folding the corners and using enough podge to fix them in place firmly.

6. Apply enough podge to the cut edge of the fabric to prevent it from fraying.

7. Apply four layers of podge over the fabric and the rest of the cabinet in different directions (from top to bottom and from left to right). Allow each layer to dry completely before applying the next.

Butterfly side table

My round pine table is old and stained and I usually cover it with a tablecloth. I wondered whether I should decoupage or mosaic it. When I started writing this book, the answer became quite clear. The large napkin images worked really well.

Before

You'll need

Table

1000- and 220-grit sandpaper

Damp cloth

Chalk paint (Annie Sloan: Provence)

Brushes

2 napkins with butterfly motif

Pair of scissors

Napkin podge

Black permanent marker

Podge – satin

1. Sand the table with 220-grit sandpaper to remove the worst marks and wipe it with a damp cloth to remove any dust.

2. Apply at least two coats of chalk paint to the entire table and allow to dry completely after each layer.

3. Carefully and neatly cut out the butterfly motifs. The butterfly feelers were too fine to cut out, so I cut them off and drew them afterwards using a black permanent marker.

4. Arrange the butterflies and mark their positions lightly in pencil.

5. Use napkin podge to fix each butterfly in place. Use your fingers to smooth out any air bubbles; work very carefully to prevent tearing the napkin. Cover the butterflies in napkin podge and allow to dry.

6. Draw the feelers and apply four layers of satin podge in different directions (from top to bottom and from left to right) over the entire table top. Allow each layer to dry completely before applying the next.

7. Sand the table top with 1000-grit sandpaper until it is smooth and dull.

8. Apply four more layers of podge as before and apply one layer of podge to the rest of the table, including the legs.

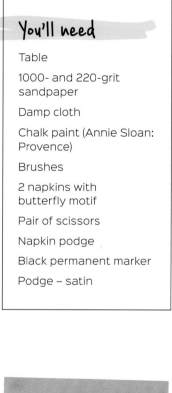

Before

Knitting corner

I found this storage box on castors and the table with its handy magazine rack in my parents' garage. In my mind's eye, I immediately saw a restored corner set. I used the same wrapping paper for both items; torn pieces on the wooden box and complete covering on the table, with a painted edge to round it off nicely.

1. Paint the inside of the storage box and the entire table with the blue chalk paint.

2. Use the compass to draw a circle on the paper, approximately 2,5 cm (1 in.) smaller than the table top, and cut out neatly.

3. Apply podge to the table, fix the circle in place in the centre and use the brayer to smooth out any air bubbles.

4. Apply four layers of podge in different directions (from top to bottom and from left to right) to the entire table top. Allow each layer to dry completely before applying the next.

5. Sand the table top with 1000-grit sandpaper until it is smooth and dull and apply four more layers of podge as before, the last layer covering the rest of the table including the legs.

6. Use a paper tearing ruler to tear a few strips of the same paper for the storage box, then tear the strips into blocks.

7. Apply podge to the sides of the box and cover them in paper blocks. Work with one side at a time and use a brayer to smooth out any air bubbles. Make sure that the corners are neat.

8. Apply four layers of podge in different directions (from top to bottom and from left to right) to the outer side edges of the box. Allow each layer to dry thoroughly before applying the next.

9. Sand the sides with 1000-grit sandpaper until the surface is smooth and dull and apply four more layers of podge as before.

10. Use wood glue to glue the wine-red ribbon to the bottom and top edge of the storage box. Allow the glue to dry and apply one layer of podge to the ribbon and all the painted areas of the box.

You'll need

Table and storage box

Chalk paint (O'Grady's: Emperors Blue)

Wrapping paper

Compass

Pair of scissors

Podge – matt

Brushes

Small brayer

Paper tearing ruler

2,5 m (2¾ yd.) wine-red ribbon (5 mm/⅕ in. wide)

Wood glue

1000-grit sandpaper

Buoy doorstopper

My sister often hikes in the beautiful Cape mountains and along its beaches. On one of these hikes, she picked up a buoy and carried it all the way so that I could do something with it for the book. What could be better than a doorstopper?

Wipe the buoy to get rid of any sand and salt, paint it with chalk paint and leave to dry completely. Neatly cut out the beach motifs, cover the back of each motif in wood glue and adhere to the buoy. Once the glue has dried, apply four layers of podge in different directions (from top to bottom and from left to right) to the buoy. Allow each layer to dry thoroughly before applying the next. Fill the buoy with pebbles so that it is heavy enough to be used as a doorstopper.

Hurricane lamp with mulberry paper

By decorating a simple hurricane lamp with handmade or textured paper, you can create a romantic corner in your house in the wink of an eye. This technique is quick and easy and suitable paper is available at most craft and stationery shops in a variety of colours and weights. This technique works best when using fairly thin paper.

Wash the glass cover and dry thoroughly. Tear the mulberry paper into small squares. Apply podge to a section of the glass and press the paper square onto the glass. It is okay for the paper to overlap slightly. Repeat until the entire glass cover is covered in paper. Apply two layers of podge in opposite directions and allow to dry after each layer. Use a craft knife to neatly trim any excess paper at the top and bottom edges.

Candles

Decoupage can transform a simple white candle into something special, such as this flower collection. Use thicker candles that will burn down the centre. Clean the candle with methylated spirits and dry thoroughly. Cut out the motifs (I used napkins), apply candle podge to the candle and carefully fix the flower motif in place while smoothing out the air bubbles with your fingers. The candle podge tends to remain sticky for quite a long time. Applying a layer of satin podge will solve this problem. I drew the outline of the arum lily with a gold permanent marker so that it would stand out against the white candle. To use heat instead of podge to adhere a napkin image, lay it over the candle, cover it with wax paper and apply heat with a hair dryer held about 2 cm (1 in.) away. The candle wax will start to melt and bleed into the napkin.

Window frame with photographs

I came across this wooden window frame at a secondhand market. The wooden frame was still solid, but the glass was scratched and damaged. The solution was to decoupage the photographs onto the glass rather than attempting to display them behind the damaged glass. The size and number of photographs you use will be determined by your specific window frame.

1. Sand the wooden frame, if necessary, and wipe away any dust using a damp cloth.

2. Apply two coats of chalk paint to the wooden frame, allow the paint to dry completely after each coat.

3. Work on a cutting mat and use the craft knife and steel ruler to trim the photographs neatly.

4. Cover the outside of the glass in a thin layer of glue and carefully position each photograph in place. Use the brayer to smooth out any air bubbles and allow the glue to dry.

5. Apply four layers of podge in different directions (from top to bottom and from left to right) to the photographs. Allow each layer to dry completely before applying the next.

6. Apply a layer of podge to the painted areas of the wooden frame to seal the paint.

You'll need

Wooden window frame

300-grit sandpaper

Chalk paint (Creative Talents: Duck Egg)

Brushes

Laser prints of 5 photographs (26 cm/10⅓ in. square) to fit your frame

Craft knife

Cutting mat

Steel ruler

Wood glue

Small brayer

Podge – matt

Photo wall

This photo wall is my favourite project in the book because it gave me the opportunity to display the wedding photographs of all my children in one collage. A photo wall takes a lot of careful planning and you must take care with your sizing and positioning to ensure that everything works together. Some photographs were pasted onto flat wooden boards and others onto canvases. Wood canvases were used to obtain different heights.

1. Determine the height and width of the section of the wall you want to cover with photographs.

2. Choose the photographs you want to use, but do not print them until you have determined their required sizes and decided on their placement.

3. Use the measurements in step 1 and do your layout on a computer if you have access to a suitable program. If not, make drawings to scale on graph paper in order to plan precisely. Determine the sizes and positions of the photographs and decide which photos are going to be used with which bases.

4. Make your laser prints of the photographs, or have them made according to the planned sizes, and neatly trim them with a craft knife. Coated paper provides the best finish. Ink prints will not work because the ink will run and prints on photo paper are not suitable because they may react to the glue and the podge.

5. Paint the sides of the canvases, as well as wooden frames that go round photograph collections, with the colour paint you have chosen. Use more than one layer if necessary.

You'll need

Photographs

Craft knife

Steel ruler

Cutting mat

Various bases for the photographs

Chalk paint (O' Grady's: Misty Grey and Sweet Lilac)

Wood glue

Brushes

Small brayer

Ribbon for selected photographs

Podge – satin

Double-sided tape (the type used to mount mirrors on a wall)

6. Apply a very thin layer of glue to the entire surface of the base on which a photograph will be pasted, position the photo accurately and use the brayer, from side to side, to smooth out any air bubbles. Be very patient and work very carefully. You do not want to make expensive mistakes when working on such a big project.

7. For variation, I finished the top and bottom of four of the photographs in ribbon to emphasise the brides' respective colour schemes.

8. Allow the glue to dry completely and place the photos in rows on a big table. Apply four layers of podge in different directions (from top to bottom and from left to right), allowing the podge to dry thoroughly after each layer.

9. Attach pieces of double-sided tape to the back of each photograph. Remove the protective layer and stick the photos onto the wall, carefully following your plan, to form the photo wall.

TIP: Alternate photographs of people with fillers that focus on décor, the cakes or even the rings.

Advent calendar

Christmas is a wonderful time of joy and togetherness and an advent calendar in the living room makes the anticipation so much more enjoyable. You can put sweets or a small gift into each drawer. This cute holder is also the ideal storage space for all your findings if you enjoy making jewellery or for small needlework accessories such as hooks and eyes, bobbins and buttons. A keen scrapbooker can use the drawers to store trimmings. Choose paper with a theme that suits the purpose of the holder.

Before

1. Paint the advent calendar with the green acrylic paint and allow to dry completely. The drawers only need to be painted on the top and sides, as the front will be covered with paper.

2. Cover the green paint in one coat of glitter paint.

3. Cut the scrapbook paper into squares to fit the drawers and use podge to paste them onto the fronts of the drawers. Do not cover the paper in podge at this stage.

4. Allow to dry and use a craft knife to neatly cut away paper in the openings of the drawers .

5. Sand the paper and paint around the edges with 300-grit sandpaper to achieve a weathered look. The more you sand, the more prominent the effect.

You'll need

Advent calendar of compressed wood

Acrylic paint (Heritage: Forest Green)

Green glitter paint

Brushes

Scrapbook paper with a Christmas theme

Craft knife

Steel ruler

Cutting mat

Podge – gloss

300-grit sandpaper

Damp cloth

Wooden numbers 1–24 to paste onto the drawers as follows: 13 x 1; 8 x 2; 3 x 3; 3 x 4; 2 x 5; 2 x 6; 2 x 7; 2 x 8; 2 x 9; 2 x 0

Wood glue

Rattan cane circle and Christmas decorations for wreath

Sweets and small gifts

6. Use a damp cloth to remove dust from the drawers and apply four layers of podge in different directions (from top to bottom and from left to right) to the fronts of the drawers. Allow each layer to dry completely before applying the next.

7. Use wood glue to stick the numbers to the drawers and cover in another layer of podge.

8. Make a Christmas wreath by winding Christmas ribbon around the rattan cane circle and covering it in podge. Allow to dry and attach Christmas decorations before fixing it in place in the middle of the advent calendar using wood glue.

9. Fill the drawers with sweets or gifts.

Christmas balls

Plain, plastic balls in various sizes are available at craft shops. They consist of two halves which can be separated if you want to decorate the inside. I used podge to apply Decopatch paper with Christmas themes and colours to the inside of the balls. It worked very well because the paper easily forms around curves. It will work just as well on the outside. Make sure that you put the paper face down when you decoupage the inside of the balls. Thread cord or ribbon, in different colours, though the eyes of the balls in order to hang them on a Christmas tree.

Cushions with feather motif

These cushion covers were made of curtain lining onto which these lovely napkins with peacock feathers were decoupaged. The fabric was decoupaged before the cushions were made and this simplified the process. I am only going to explain the decoupage technique and not how to make the cushion.

You'll need

Fabric for the cushions

Pair of scissors

Teflon craft mat

Napkins with peacock feather motif

Napkin podge

Soft brush

Podge – satin

1. Cut the fabric for the cushions slightly bigger than the size of the napkin.

2. Separate the napkin layers because you only use the top layer.

3. Work on the Teflon craft mat. Work from side to side. Apply a strip of napkin podge to the fabric and carefully press the napkin onto the podge.

4. Apply another strip of podge and press the napkin onto the podge. Work in strips until the whole napkin has been transferred to the material. Be patient and work carefully so that the napkin does not tear.

5. Apply four layers of napkin podge in different directions (from top to bottom and from left to right) to the napkin. Allow each layer to dry completely before applying the next.

6. Apply two layers of satin podge to the napkin podge because the latter tends to stay a bit sticky. Allow the first layer to dry completely before applying the second.

7. Leave the podge to dry completely before finishing the cushion covers.

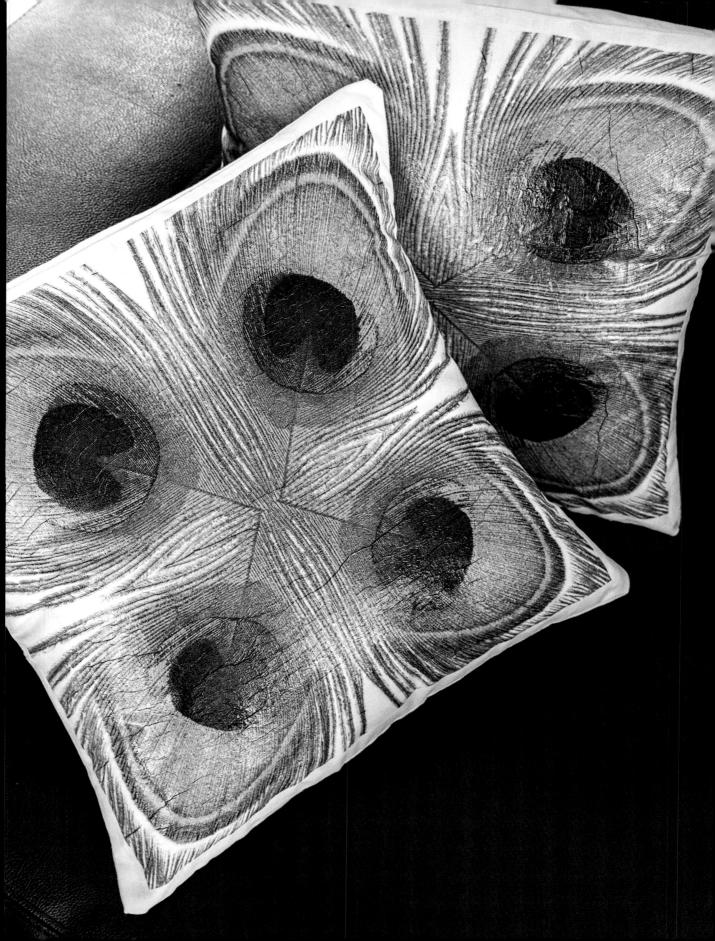

Tins galore

Before

Tins are one of the easiest items to decoupage. Every technique discussed in the book can be applied to tins. Because tins come in different shapes and sizes, you can make beautiful gifts by découpaging tins and filling them with titbits, toiletries, stationery or something similar. The tins are both decorative and functional. If the original colour of the tin is dark, apply a coat of white spray paint before applying other colours or decorating it with decoupage.

You can cover a tin completely or you can decorate it with motifs and napkins.

Leftover pieces of paper from other projects can also be used. Raffia, ribbon, Washi tape, braid, etcetera can give a lovely finish to any decoupaged tin. The possibilities are endless. Use your imagination and create tins that reflect your creativity.

The basic requirements for all the tins are spray paint, paper, podge and brushes.

Photograph on tin

You do not have to stick to decoupage paper or wrapping paper when you decoupage. This interesting photograph of tree roots was printed on matt paper using a laser printer and it really stands out on the tin that was spray painted white. The top edge of the tin was finished with raffia, glued in place and covered with podge. A section of the print had to be cut off for the rest to fit around the tin, and this was decoupaged onto the lid. As usual, everything was covered in four layers of podge applied in different directions. Photographs of grandchildren will be great on a tin for grandparents and will be striking in black and white.

Angel tins

The round and oval tins were first painted with white spray paint and then the tall oval tin was painted with acrylic paint – Beryl Blue. I used only one coat of blue to achieve the streaky look. The six-sided tin was originally this pretty turquoise colour and was merely decorated with paper and podge.

Matt podge was used to attach the pictures to the tins, after which each tin and lid was covered in four layers of podge applied in different directions. The lids were also decorated with motifs from the same decoupage paper. All the motifs came from the same sheet of paper and the collection of tins makes for a lovely focal point.

Pink and turquoise tins

The striking, bright colours are the result of Decopatch paper that was applied over a layer of white spray paint. One of the advantages of Decopatch paper is the bold colours that remain bold even when podge is applied to the paper. It is great fun putting together a variety of print patterns in a several shades. A teenager will find a set of these tins ideal for storing her knick-knacks.

All the tins were completely covered in Decopatch paper to which matt podge was applied. Thin Washi tape was used as a finishing touch on the smaller tins. The Decopatch paper moulded neatly around the lip of the lid, which is what makes working with this paper such a pleasure. Four layers of satin podge were applied in different directions to the tins and lids.

For the wooden box, the Decopatch paper was cut into squares and arranged in a random, yet orderly fashion. Matt podge was used to fix them in place on the lid and the base of the box. The inside was also decoupaged, giving it a neat finish. The box and lid were then covered in four layers of podge applied in different directions.

A touch of gold

One of these tins had a gold base, another had a gold lid and I painted the third one's base gold so that I could use it in the set. The pretty jewel-coloured Decopatch paper really suited the opulent gold. This paper is thin and easily moulds around the curves of the lids when you fix it in place with podge. For the purple lid of the round tin, Decopatch paper was cut into squares and affixed with podge to give the lid an interesting texture. They overlap slightly to ensure complete cover. The tin in the middle was completely covered in Decopatch paper that matched the gold lid. A gold permanent marker was used to colour in the upper lip to ensure uninterrupted flow between the base and the lid. Four layers of podge were applied to the paper.

Tins with world-map paper

The octagonal tin was painted with white spray paint and the round ones with leaf-green acrylic paint. The paper covers the tins completely and the same paper was cut to size to decorate just the centre of the octagonal lid.

Irrespective of how the tins are decorated, two to four layers of podge applied in different directions will produce the best finish.

Kitchen stools

These kitchen stools are more than 20 years old and I have been itching to revamp them. With a little paint and Decopatch paper, the chairs underwent a complete transformation. The original colour was fairly dark, so I applied a coat of white PVA before applying the new colour.

Before

1. Sand the stools with 220-grit sandpaper to get rid of old varnish and blemishes, wipe with a damp cloth to remove all the dust and apply one coat of white PVA.

2. Allow the paint to dry completely before applying the colour. Alternate the two shades of blue between the legs and the rails.

3. Paint the underside of the stool seats with one of the blues and leave to dry completely.

4. Cut the Decopatch paper into rectangles and squares of various sizes. Apply podge to a section of the seat and arrange the paper randomly, yet in an orderly fashion, on the podge. Cover the paper in podge and repeat until the top and side are covered in paper. Allow to dry.

5. Apply four more layers of podge in different directions (from top to bottom and from left to right) and allow to dry thoroughly between layers.

6. Apply high gloss varnish to the entire chair once the podge is completely dry.

You'll need

Chairs

White PVA

220-grit sandpaper

Separate brushes for paint and podge

Acrylic paint (I used Heritage: Beryl Blue and Bright Blue)

Decopatch paper in shades of green and blue for the seats

Pair of scissors

Podge – gloss

High gloss varnish

TIP: Decopatch paper is ideal for projects where the paper needs to be podged around curves. You can also use napkins, but do not cut them.

Vegetable crate

Before

Although this old raw-wood crate had a charm of its own, I sanded it and finished it with paint and podge so that it can be used to store vegetables. It will be very easy to make your own crate by sawing wooden planks into the right sizes and gluing them together.

1. Thoroughly sand the crate with 220-grit sandpaper. Lightly sweep your hand over the crate to make sure that there are no splinters that may prick you when you use it. Use a damp cloth to remove all the dust.

2. Paint the inside of the crate with two coats of acrylic paint. Allow each coat to dry completely before applying a layer of podge.

3. Use the chalk paint to apply a colour wash finish (see page 21) to the outside and bottom of the crate and leave to dry thoroughly.

4. Carefully cut out the vegetable motifs that you wish to use and arrange them on the outside of the crate. Use podge to glue the motifs in place once you are satisfied with your arrangement.

5. Apply at least four layers of podge to the outside and bottom of the crate, working in different directions and leaving each layer to dry completely before applying the next.

You'll need

Raw-wood crate

220-grit sandpaper

Damp cloth

Acrylic paint (Heritage: Bone White)

Chalk paint (Fired Earth: French Clay)

Podge – matt

Brushes

Decoupage paper with vegetable motif

Pair of scissors

Craft knife

Cutting mat

Egg box

Eggs used for baking must be at room temperature. This dinky compressed-wood egg box is ideal for eggs that are not going into the fridge and, if decoupaged, it doubles up as a kitchen decoration. This box holds 12 eggs but smaller boxes that hold six eggs are also available at craft shops.

Before

1. Unscrew the door of the egg box and set aside the hinges where you will find them again.

2. Apply two coats of acrylic paint to the box and the door, allowing the first coat to dry before applying the second.

3. Stick masking tape right around the box just below the upper hinge mark and just above the lower hinge mark, as well as on the corresponding parts of the door.

4. Apply two coats of chalk paint between the two strips of masking tape and to the top of the box. Allow to dry thoroughly after each coat and carefully remove the masking tape once the paint has dried completely.

5. Carefully cut out the motif you have chosen and use napkin podge to position the motif on the box. Use the brayer to smooth out any air bubbles before covering the box and door in a layer of podge. Allow to dry.

6. Decorate the egg box with Washi tape as shown in the photograph, or to your own liking, and apply at least four layers of satin podge to the entire box (including the Washi tape).

7. Replace the door when the podge is completely dry.

You'll need

Egg box made of MDF

Small Phillips screwdriver

Brushes

Acrylic paint (Heritage: Bone White)

Chalk paint (Heritage: Olivia)

Masking tape

Napkin podge

Podge – satin

Pair of scissors

Craft knife

Cutting mat

Small brayer

Napkin with chicken motif

Washi tape (red and white stripes 1 cm (^{2}/5 in.) wide, turquoise 0,5 cm (1/5 in.) wide)

Grey and white pot stand

There is room for pot stands in every kitchen. I used Washi tape and a paint wash to decorate a number of same-size wooden blocks that have been lying around my house for ages. I then glued them to a wooden base and applied satin varnish to seal them and make them heat resistant.

You'll need

20 wooden blocks of 2,5 x 11,5 x 0,5 cm (1 x 4½ x ⅕ in.)

25 cm (10 in.) wooden square, 0,2 cm (⅕ in.) thick

2 wooden slats of 24 x 2 x 2 cm (9½ x ⅘ x ⅘ in.)

White acrylic paint

Brushes

Washi tape in 5 different designs (I used shades of grey and white)

Decu varnish satin

Wood glue

Pair of scissors

1. Cover eight of the 20 small blocks in a thin coat of white acrylic paint that has been diluted 1:1 with water. Do not dilute too much paint; you need very little because the wood grain must shine through.

2. Apply undiluted paint to the 25 cm (10 in.) square block and the two longer wooden slats. Allow to dry and apply a second coat of paint if necessary.

3. Decorate the remaining 12 small blocks with Washi tape, alternating the designs across the width of each block.

4. Use wood glue to glue the blocks onto the wooden square in a basket-weave pattern, leaving a border all around. Allow to dry.

5. Glue the two wooden slats to the bottom of the wooden square to form the feet of the pot stand and allow to dry.

6. Cover the top in at least eight coats of satin varnish. Apply them in different directions, leaving each coat to dry thoroughly before applying the next. This makes the pot stand heat and water resistant.

TIP: You can glue four big wooden beads to the bottom of the wooden square to serve as feet for the pot-rest.

Cutlery caddy

A friend gave me this useful caddy filled with sauces. Having used the sauces I decided to give it a new look and use it for cutlery. It is also suitable for other condiments.

Before

1. To create a distressed look, sand the caddy with 600-grit sandpaper to remove most of the white paint and use a damp cloth to remove the dust.

2. Separate the layers of the napkins so that you will work with only one layer of each. Use napkin podge to affix a napkin to opposite sides of the caddy. Use the brayer to smooth out the air bubbles and allow the podge to dry thoroughly. Two sides will be podged and two sides will not be podged.

3. Use a craft knife to trim the sides neatly.

4. Apply at least four layers of satin podge in opposite directions over the napkins and the rest of the holder. Allow to dry completely after each layer.

5. Sand the caddy with 1000-grit sandpaper and apply another four layers of podge.

You'll need

Wooden caddy with four compartments

600-grit sandpaper

2 napkins with rose motif

Napkin podge

Podge – satin

Brushes

Pair of scissors

Craft knife

Small brayer

1000-grit sandpaper

Soup mugs with lace

Simple soup or coffee mugs can be decorated with lace or ribbon to create a unique look. If you cover the lace or ribbon in CPG podge and bake it in an oven, the mug can be washed in warm, soapy water. I suggest you steer clear of a dishwasher, though.

1. Use wood glue to glue the lace to the mugs. It dries clear. Make sure that you apply enough glue to the overlapping edges.

2. Allow the glue to dry completely. Apply six layers of CPG podge to the lace. Each layer must be completely dry before the next is applied. To prevent tears from forming, don't use too much podge at one go.

3. Set the mugs aside until the podge has dried completely.

4. Heat the oven to 90 °C (194 °F) and bake the mugs in the oven for one hour.

5. If the podge has run a little or formed tears, use a craft knife to scrape it off carefully.

You'll need

Soup mugs

Lace

Wood glue

CPG podge

Brush

Pair of scissors

Red and white utensil holder

Once I got going with the red and white theme for kitchen items, there was no stopping me. I painted and decoupaged a wooden utensil holder using Decopatch paper which is very easy to use and is especially effective when working with curves.

You'll need

Utensil holder

Acrylic paint – white

Brushes

Decopatch paper with red and white motifs

Pair of scissors

Podge – matt

1. Apply one coat of paint to the inside and outside of the holder and allow to dry.

2. Cut the Decopatch paper into squares of various sizes. Cover the holder with podge and stick down the squares randomly, overlapping to cover the entire holder. Use the brush to achieve a neat finish at the top and bottom edges and smooth out any air bubbles with your fingers.

3. Apply at least four layers of matt podge in different directions, making sure that each layer is completely dry before applying the next.

Red and white pot plant covers

Ordinary plastic covers for pot plants are readily available in shops. I bought a number of these covers and decorated them in a jiffy by covering them in sheets of Decopatch paper using podge. The paper design echoes the covers' scalloped edge. After the paper was podged over the entire cover, the scallops were neatly cut out using a craft knife on a cutting mat. The podge stiffens the paper when dry, which makes it easy to cut the edges accurately. Four layers of podge were applied in opposite directions over the paper. It is advisable to use podge that is suitable for outdoor use (outdoor podge) so that the covers can also be used outside.

Round red tray

Many people probably have one of these round plastic trays in their kitchen. This one was dull and scratched on the inside and was just gathering dust in a corner. A pretty appliqué tray cloth provided just the facelift it needed and I used podge to fix it in place. The result is an attractive tray that can be cleaned with a wet cloth.

Clean the tray with a damp cloth to get rid of any dust and dirt before you fix the cloth in place with the podge. Allow to dry thoroughly and apply four layers of gloss podge in different directions over the cloth. Make sure that each layer is completely dry before applying the next.

Chicken tray

Galvanized metal items in various shapes and sizes are readily available and very popular as a base for decoupage. Watering cans, pots, wash basins, waste-paper baskets, buckets, trays and pans are stocked by florists, craft and décor shops. These decorated items can be both decorative and functional because they are sealed with podge.

1. Apply two coats of chalk paint to the inside and outside of the pan. Make sure that the first coat is completely dry before applying the second.

2. Carefully cut out the chicken motifs. Use a craft knife to cut out the finer details before cutting along the outside edges. Separate the layers of the napkin and only use the top layer.

3. Arrange the motifs and make a light pencil mark where you want them before sticking them in place with the napkin podge. Use a soft brush and work very carefully so that the napkin does not tear.

4. Use a brayer to smooth out the air bubbles and use a damp cloth to remove excess podge.

5. Immediately apply a layer of napkin podge to the motifs and allow to dry thoroughly.

6. Cover the entire tray in four layers of satin podge applied in different directions. Allow each layer to dry before applying the next.

7. Sand the tray with 1000-grit sandpaper and apply another four layers of podge as before.

You'll need

Galvanized metal tray

Chalk paint (Harlequin: Aged White)

Brushes

Napkins with chicken motif

Pair of scissors

Craft knife

Cutting mat

Pencil

Podge – satin

Napkin podge

Small brayer

Damp cloth

1000-grit sandpaper

Espresso tray

This beautiful espresso tray can be decorative as well as functional. When not in use, it can be displayed in the kitchen as a focal point. The resin finish gives it a beautiful shine.

Before

1. Apply two coats of acrylic paint to the inside and outside of the tray. Allow to dry completely between layers.

2. Carefully cut out the motifs you want to use, arrange them on the tray and make light pencil marks where each one must be placed.

3. Use podge to fix the motifs in place on the tray. Use the brayer to smooth out all the air bubbles, apply podge to the rest of the tray and leave to dry completely.

4. Prepare the resin according to the product instructions and pour it over the motifs on the tray (see page 25).

5. Set the tray aside under a suitable covering until the resin is completely cured (at least 24 hours).

6. Finish off the edges of the tray by drawing a border using the gold marker.

7. Glue the cork sheet to the bottom of the tray.

You'll need

Wooden (MDF) tray

Red acrylic paint (Heritage: Tomato red)

Brushes

Decoupage paper

Pair of scissors

Pencil

Podge – matt

Small brayer

Gold marker

Resin (Heritage: Liquid glass)

Cork sheet

Wood glue

Red and white dishcloth hanger

When I came across this beautiful paper with a kitchen theme I just had to find some way to use it. My husband made me a dishcloth hanger using a couple of planks, and the motifs on the paper could be displayed to their full potential.

1. Apply two coats of white acrylic paint to the hanger. Allow the first coat to dry completely before applying the second.

2. Carefully cut out the motifs you want to use and decide how you want to arrange them on the hanger. Mark the selected positions in pencil.

3. Apply podge to the hanger and glue the motifs in place. Do not trim the motifs where they cover the open spaces between the planks just yet.

4. Use the brayer to smooth out all air bubbles.

5. Apply four layers of satin podge in different directions over the front of the hanger. Allow each layer to dry completely before applying the next.

6. Sand the front with 1000-grit sandpaper and apply four layers of podge as before.

7. Turn the hanger over and carefully cut out the paper between the openings using a craft knife and working on a cutting mat

8. Screw the hooks into the bottom plank at equal distances.

You'll need

Dishcloth hanger –
3 planks of
10 x 45 x 0,5 cm
(4 x 18 x ⅕ in.) nailed onto
2 slats of 4 x 42 x 0,8 cm
(1³⁄₅ x 16½ x ½ in.)

Acrylic paint – white

Brushes

Decoupage paper with kitchen theme

Pair of scissors

Craft knife

Cutting mat

Pencil

Podge – satin

1000-grit sandpaper

Small brayer

3 screw-in hooks

Red and white tin

This lovely tin was decoupaged with the same paper as the dishcloth hanger and together they form a pretty unit in the kitchen. Fill it with rusks or biscuits and it becomes an ideal gift.

1. Spray the tin and lid with white spray paint and allow to dry completely.

2. Carefully cut out the motifs you want to use on the tin, arrange them and mark the selected positions in pencil.

3. Apply podge and glue the motifs in place on the tin. Use the brayer to smooth out any air bubbles and leave to dry.

4. Apply at least four layers of satin podge in different directions, making sure that each layer is completely dry before applying the next.

You'll need

Tin

White spray paint

Decoupage paper

Pair of scissors

Craft mat

Pencil

Podge – satin

Brush

Small brayer

Lazy Susan

This lazy Susan with its fresh, bright colours is ideal for a cheerful breakfast table. Between meals it can host a vase of fresh flowers to brighten your kitchen. There is a large variety of kitchen specific decoupage paper available in stores and you can mix and match motifs for kitchen items to your heart's delight.

Before

1. Apply at least two coats of white paint to the lazy Susan; make sure that each coat is completely dry before applying the next.

2. Carefully cut out the motifs you want to use. First cut out the fine details using a craft knife before cutting along the outer edges.

3. Arrange the motifs on the lazy Susan. Use a pencil to mark the spots where the motifs must be placed.

4. Apply podge to the surface, fix each motif in place and use the brayer to smooth out any air bubbles.

5. Apply at least four layers of satin podge in different directions; allow podge to dry completely between layers.

6. Sand the surface with 1000-grit sandpaper until it is completely dull.

7. Remove any dust with a damp cloth and apply four more layers of podge as before.

8. Use wood glue to adhere the ribbon around the edge of the lazy Susan. Coat with a layer of podge once the glue is completely dry.

You'll need

Lazy Susan blank (MDF)

Acrylic paint (Heritage: Warm White)

Brushes

Decoupage paper

Pair of scissors

Craft knife

Cutting mat

Pencil

Podge – satin

Brayer

1000-grit sandpaper

1,2 m (1⅓ yd.) ribbon, 1 cm (⅖ in.) wide (enough to go round the lazy Susan)

Wood glue

Blue and white placemats

I found this set of placemats at the annual sale of a department store. They were a good size and non-slip, but I did not like the pattern on them. I decoupaged them with blue and white wrapping paper that was thick enough to hide the original pattern.

1. Cut the wrapping paper slightly bigger than the placemat.

2. Cover the surface of the placemat in podge and carefully place the paper on it. Starting in the middle of the placemat, flatten out the paper with your fingers and use the brayer to smooth out any air bubbles.

3. Leave the podge to dry, place the placemat upside down on a cutting mat and carefully trim the excess paper using a craft knife (see page 24).

4. Apply at least four layers of podge in different directions; make sure that each layer is completely dry before applying the next.

You'll need

Placemats made of compressed wood

Wrapping paper

Pair of scissors

Podge – matt

Brush

Small brayer

Craft knife

Cutting mat

Owl teabag tin

This tin has an unusual shape and is just the right size for storing teabags. The owl napkins have been waiting in my craft cupboard for the right base and the paper flower cut outs are a perfect match for them. I painted the lid green but it will also look pretty with decoupaged motifs.

1. Spray the tin and the lid with the white spray paint, allow to dry and paint the lid with the green acrylic paint.

2. Carefully cut out the owl motifs and separate the layers of the napkin.

3. Use podge to fix the motifs in place on the tin; use a soft brush and work carefully so that you do not tear the napkin.

4. Punch flowers out of the coloured paper, use satin podge to fix them in place on the tin and leave to dry.

5. Apply at least four layers of matt podge to the tin and the lid. Work in opposite directions and make sure that each layer is completely dry before applying the next.

6. Use wood glue to glue the ribbon in place around the bottom of the tin. Coat the ribbon with one layer of podge as soon as the glue is completely dry.

You'll need

Tin

White spray paint

Acrylic paint (Heritage: Leaf Green)

Napkin with owl motifs

Pair of scissors

Craft knife

Cutting mat

Napkin podge

Soft brush

Podge – matt

Wood glue

Ribbon to go around tin

Flower punch

Coloured paper in matching colours

Headboard

This headboard and mirror date back to the seventies when cane furniture was very popular. Both were still in a very good condition but needed a make-over. It was tough going getting rid of the varnish, but it was well worth the effort. The framework was given a distressed look and curtain fabric was used for the arches. The advantage that this has over an upholstered headboard, is that the podge is waterproof and any dirty marks can simply be removed with a wet cloth.

Before

You'll need

Headboard and mirror

Sanding machine

Damp cloth

Chalk paint (Harlequin: Aged White)

Brushes

220-grit sandpaper

Dark brown wax

Soft cloth

Mounting-board – enough for arches

Craft knife

Steel ruler

Cutting mat

Fabric – enough to cover mounting-board

Pair of scissors

Podge – matt

Small brayer

Wood glue

Cord to finish the inserts

1. Use sandpaper to remove as much of the varnish from the headboard and mirror as possible. My husband assisted me by using an electric sanding machine to get rid of the varnish. If you do not have access to a sanding machine, use 220-grit sandpaper.

2. Wipe the furniture with a damp cloth to remove all the dust left after the sanding and apply at least two layers of chalkboard paint. Make sure that each layer is completely dry before applying the next.

3. Sand the paint here and there to create a distressed look.

4. Apply dark brown wax to the paint and polish it immediately with a soft cloth. Work on small areas at a time and do not apply wax to a large section before polishing. Wax that lies on the paint for too long before being polished, makes the paint too dark.

5. Cut mounting-board into arches that will fit perfectly into the plaited inserts of the headboard. The arches will not necessarily be exactly the same size or shape.

6. Cut out fabric arches big enough to cover the mounting board allowing 1,5 cm (³/₅ in.) all round to fold over to the back.

7. Apply podge to the mounting-board and affix fabric to it. Use the brayer to smooth out air bubbles. Turn the mounting-board over and cut notches at the curves so that the fabric can be neatly shaped around them. Use podge to fix the folded-over pieces in place and apply a layer of podge over them.

8. Apply four layers of podge in different directions (from top to bottom and from left to right) to the front of the arches. Allow each layer to dry completely before applying the next.

9. Use wood glue to affix the mounting-boards to the headboard. Place it flat on the floor with heavy objects such as books on top while the glue dries to ensure that the mounting-boards are firmly stuck in place.

10. Use wood glue to stick cord around the arches to finish them off. Cover the cord in a layer of podge.

Chair with lace seat

Before

An old office chair is an ideal candidate for restoration. This chair has a sturdy frame and seat. The ugly imitation leather seat was decoupaged with lace. This complimented the frame which was sanded and painted with chalk paint, creating a distressed paint finish.

1. Remove the seat of the chair and sand the frame to remove any varnish.

2. Wipe with a damp cloth and apply at least two coats of chalk paint. Make sure that each layer dries completely.

3. Sand the chair here and there to create a distressed look.

4. Apply clear wax to the frame and leave to dry. Polish it with a soft cloth to give the chair a satin finish.

5. Cut a piece of lace big enough to cover the seat and fold over its underside.

6. Use podge to stick the lace to the seat. Use the brush to force the podge into the holes of the lace. You have to just about drench the lace in the podge; if you do not apply enough podge, the lace will come loose easily. Only do the top of the seat.

7. When the top is completely dry (it can take up to two days to dry), you can fold the lace over the underside, affixing it with podge.

8. Stick drawing pins into the lace or staple the lace under the seat to ensure that it is firmly held in place.

You'll need

Chair

600-grit sandpaper

Chalk paint (Heritage: Crème Brûlée)

Brushes

Clear wax

Soft cloth

Lace for seat

Pair of scissors

Podge – matt

Drawing-pins or staple gun

Bedside lamps

The beautiful shape of the pedestals of these bedside lamps made me feel obliged to restore them. The heat from the bulbs had made their distinctive parchment lampshades, with real leather riempies, hard and brittle. I decided to restore the lampshades rather than buying new ones. One lampshade was decoupaged with the same lace as the office chair and the other with hessian. I made a collage for the pedestals using words from various languages meaning "sleep well" and printed it on 80-gsm paper.

Before

You'll need

Bedside lamps

Printed paper with words

Podge – satin

Pair of scissors

Unbleached linen
(1 m/1,1 yd.) for the inside

Lace (approximately
0,5 m/⅝ yd.) for the
outside

Hessian (approximately
0,5 m/⅝ yd.) for the
outside

Craft knife

Steel ruler

Cutting mat

Bulldog clip

Ribbon matching the
lace (2 m/2⅕ yd.)

Twine matching the
hessian (2 m/2⅕ yd.)

Wood glue

Bulldog clip

Pedestals

1. Cut the paper into squares and rectangles of various sizes. Use podge to paste them onto the pedestals in different directions and overlapping slightly.

2. Use your fingers to smooth out any air bubbles – the pieces of paper are small enough.

3. Once the whole pedestal is covered in paper, apply four layers of podge in different directions (from top to bottom and from left to right). Allow each layer to dry completely before applying the next.

4. Use a craft knife to neatly trim the paper at the top and bottom edges of the pedestal.

Lampshades

1. Carefully remove each lampshade from its frame and loosen it at the join so that it can be laid flat.

2. Cut the unbleached linen to size to cover the lampshades. Apply podge to the inside of the lampshade and press the unbleached linen firmly onto the podge. Use the brayer to smooth out any air bubbles.

3. Apply at least four layers of podge over the fabric; allow the podge to dry thoroughly between layers and neatly trim excess fabric.

4. Cut the lace and hessian to size to cover the respective lampshades. Apply podge to the outside of the lampshade and press the lace/hessian firmly in place. Use the brayer to smooth out any air bubbles.

5. Apply four layers of podge in different directions (from top to bottom and from left to right) to the outside of the lampshade. Allow each layer to dry completely before applying the next. Trim the excess fabric.

6. Use a craft knife to open the holes for threading the ribbon or twine.

7. Fold the lampshades back into shape and use wood glue to join the edges, keeping them in place with bulldog clips or something similar until the glue is completely dry. Attach the shades to their frames by threading the ribbon or twine through the holes.

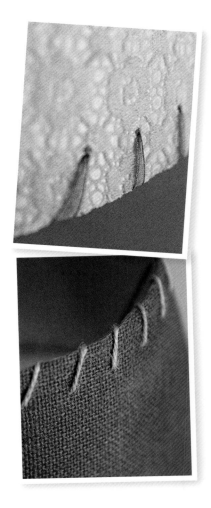

Jewellery box

I cannot resist a bargain, so I just had to buy this jewellery box on a sale. It was white, had marks on it that I could not remove and the lid was decorated with beads and metal that I found garish. I used paint and wax to create a distressed look and replaced the beads and metal with vintage pictures on the inside and outside of the lid.

1. Remove the hinges and clasp of the jewellery box. (The feet could not be removed because they were stuck to the box.)

2. Lightly sand the box to give the surface a rough texture. Apply two coats of dark pink chalk paint to the inside and outside. Make sure that the first coat is completely dry before applying the second.

3. Apply one coat of the lighter chalk paint to the outside and the lid and allow to dry until the paint feels dry to the touch.

4. Apply clear wax to the paint and polish immediately with a soft cloth. You will find that you can wipe away quite a bit of the top coat of paint during the polishing process. Keep polishing until you achieve the desired effect.

5. Use wood glue to paste the pictures onto the cardboard, leave the glue to dry and apply two layers of podge to the pictures in different directions; allow each layer to dry completely.

6. Apply two base layers of crackle varnish in different directions (from left to right and from top to bottom) to the pictures. Wait for the first layer to dry before applying the second.

7. Leave the second layer to dry completely before applying the top coat. The cracks will begin to appear while the top coat dries. It takes at least five hours to dry completely and it is advisable to leave it to dry overnight.

8. Rub a little of the dark chalk paint into the cracks and polish the pictures with wax.

9. Use wood glue to affix the pictures to the top and inside of the lid and replace the hinges and clasp.

Vintage chest of drawers

Before

This chest of drawers was the middle section of a big wardrobe in one of our bedrooms. We got rid of the other sections but always found a space for the chest of drawers with its useful mirror. The beautiful wrapping paper decoupaged onto the drawers and the exceptional colour chalk paint gave the chest a vintage look, and it is now a focal point in our guest bedroom.

You'll need

Chest of drawers

Screwdriver

Chalk paint (Chiswick: Flamingo)

Brushes

Podge – satin

Wrapping paper with vintage theme

Craft knife

Steel ruler

Cutting mat

Small brayer

300-grit sandpaper

Pair of scissors

Transfer glaze

1. Unscrew the drawer and door knobs and remove the drawers.

2. Paint the sides of the chest and the outside of the drawers with the chalk paint. Apply two coats and make sure that the first coat is completely dry before applying the second.

3. Apply two layers of podge to the chalk paint to prevent it from being scratched. Make sure that the first layer is completely dry before applying the second.

4. Measure the front part of the drawers and the top door of the chest and cut strips of wrapping paper slightly smaller. Use a steel ruler and craft knife for straight edges. Try to cut the paper so that the pattern continues from one drawer to the next.

5. Apply podge to the front of each drawer and affix the paper. Use the brayer to smooth out any air bubbles. Repeat with the top door.

6. Allow to dry, then lightly sand the edges of the drawers and door with sandpaper to achieve a distressed finish.

7. Apply four layers of podge in different directions (from top to bottom and from left to right) to the paper. Allow each layer to dry completely before applying the next.

8. Decorate the knobs as described on page 27 by using transfer glaze and screw them in place on the drawers and door.

Pallet wood heart

Blanks made of raw wood or pallets are readily available at most craft and hardware stores or you can make them yourself. This wooden heart with its raw wood slats immediately grabbed my attention and I loved using decoupage to turn it into a beautiful jewellery hanger.

1. Sand the heart with 300-grit sandpaper and make sure that the surface is fairly smooth.

2. Wipe the heart with a damp cloth to remove all the dust.

3. Alternate the three chalk paint colours and colourwash the different slats of the wooden heart (see page 21). Use very little paint and lots of water. You can always add a little paint if the colour is not bright enough. Allow the wood to dry completely.

4. Cut out the rose motifs and separate the layers of the napkin. You only use the top layer.

5. Affix the rose motifs to the heart using napkin podge and carefully smooth out any air bubbles using your fingers. Do not rub too hard because the napkin can easily tear. Apply a layer of podge over the motifs. Do not cut the rose motif where it is positioned over two slats.

6. Apply two layers of satin podge in opposite directions over the entire heart allowing to dry completely after each layer.

7. Using a craft knife, carefully cut through the rose motif where it is positioned over two slats.

8. Position the hooks randomly on the heart and attach the screw to the back to secure the pink cord and ribbon for hanging the heart on the wall.

You'll need

Pallet wood heart

300-grit sandpaper

Damp cloth

Chalk paint (O'Grady's: Misty Grey, Grey Violet and Sweet Lilac)

Brushes

Napkin with rose motif

Pair of scissors

Craft knife

Cutting mat

Napkin podge

Podge – satin

Pink ribbon and cord

3 screw-in hooks

1 screw

Pallet wall clock

When I came across a craft kit containing this pallet wood clock with mechanism I snapped it up because it was a perfect companion for the pallet heart. I finished it using the same theme as for the heart. The colour of the hands did not go with my colour scheme, but gold spray paint was an easy solution to this problem.

1. Sand the round wooden board and make sure that the surface is fairly smooth.

2. Wipe the board with a damp cloth to remove all the dust.

3. Alternate the three chalk paint colours and colourwash the different slats of the wooden board (see page 21). Use very little paint and lots of water. You can always add a little paint if the colour is not bright enough. Allow the wood to dry completely.

4. Cut out the rose motifs and separate the layers of the napkin. You only use the top layer.

5. Affix the rose motifs to the boards/slats using napkin podge and carefully smooth out any air bubbles using your fingers. Do not rub too hard because the napkin can easily tear. Apply a layer of podge over the motifs. Do not cut rose motifs positioned over two slats.

6. Apply two layers of satin podge in opposite directions over all the slats allowing to dry completely after each layer.

7. Using a craft knife, carefully cut through rose motifs positioned over the slats.

8. Attach the clock mechanism and hands to the centre slat.

9. Attach the screw to the back to secure the twine for hanging the clock on the wall.

You'll need

Pallet wood circle

300-grit sandpaper

Damp cloth

Chalk paint (O'Grady's: Misty Grey, Grey Violet and Sweet Lilac)

Brushes

Napkin with rose motif

Craft knife

Cutting mat

Pair of scissors

Napkin podge

Podge – satin

Clock mechanism and hands

Screw

Twine to hang clock

Wall tiles podged with scarf

I am crazy about scarves – I wear them in summer and winter – and have a huge variety. The scarf I used for this project was one of my favourites, but it had seen better days. Using it for this project was much better than throwing it away. You can repurpose any clothing items with sentimental value in this way. A friend of mine decoupaged tiles using pieces of fabric from her late mom's dresses to create a pretty mosaic artwork. The tiles I used were leftovers from other projects. Use what you have at home.

1. Cut the scarf or fabric to size to cover the tiles and fold over the edges.

2. Apply a thin layer of wood glue to each tile and firmly press the fabric in place. Use the brayer to smooth out any air bubbles.

3. Neatly fold the corners, fold the fabric over and stick it to the back of the tiles.

4. When the glue has dried completely, apply four layers of podge in different directions (from top to bottom and from right to left) over the fabric; allow each layer to dry thoroughly before applying the next.

5. Sand the surface with 1000-grit sandpaper to achieve a smooth finish. Wipe the surface to get rid of any dust and apply four more layers of podge as before.

6. Attach double-sided tape to the back of the tiles, remove the backing layer and firmly affix the tiles to the wall in an arrangement of your choice.

You'll need

Scarf or pretty fabric

Pair of scissors

3 large glazed tiles of 20 x 30 cm

5 small glazed tiles of 5 x 5 cm

Wood glue

Small brayer

Podge – satin

1000-grit sandpaper

Double-sided tape (the type used to mount mirrors on a wall)

Growth chart

Creating décor for a child's room is easy because there is such a wide variety of paper to choose from. My grandson is crazy about aeroplanes and trains, so I chose aeroplane paper for this growth chart. You can make it any colour to match your colour scheme.

1. Apply two coats of acrylic paint to the canvas and allow to dry completely after each coat.

2. Use wood glue to stick the measuring tape 2,5 cm (1 in.) from one of the long edges of the canvas. Start it at approximately 20 cm (8 in.) at the bottom, so that the height chart can be positioned away from the floor.

3. Carefully cut out the aeroplane motifs and arrange on the canvas.

4. Use podge to stick the aeroplanes onto the canvas, smoothing out any air bubbles with your fingers or the small brayer.

5. Apply four layers of podge in different directions (from top to bottom and from left to right) to the canvas. Allow each layer to dry completely before applying the next.

6. Attach double-sided tape to the back of the canvas close to the edges. Remove the backing tape and firmly affix the height chart to the wall, 20 cm (8 in.) from the floor.

You'll need

Flat canvas of 125 x 18 cm (50 x 7¼ in.)

Acrylic paint (Heritage: Beryl Blue)

Brushes

Fabric measuring tape

Wood glue

Wrapping paper with aeroplane motifs

Pair of scissors

Pencil

Podge – gloss

Small brayer

Double-sided tape

Toy box

Unfortunately we never took a picture of this toy box before I decoupaged it! The rather unsightly plastic box was stuck away in a cupboard. After it was painted and decoupaged, it became a cheerful focal point in my grandson's bedroom. He can easily open the lid, take his toys out and put them back. Trains are Arno's other favourite and the fabric with these gorgeous train motifs just about jumped into my hands!

1. Spray paint the entire box and leave to dry.

2. Cut the fabric to size to fit the sides and the lid of the toy box.

3. Use podge to affix the fabric to the toy box and smooth out any air bubbles with the brayer.

4. Apply four layers of podge in different directions (from top to bottom and from left to right) to the sides and the lid of the box. Allow each layer to dry completely before applying the next.

5. Make sure that the cut edges of the fabric are completely covered in podge to prevent them from fraying.

You'll need

Toy box

Spray paint that sticks to all surfaces (Painter's Touch: Ultra Cover)

Fabric with suitable motifs

Pair of scissors

Podge – gloss

Brush

Small brayer

Nursery organiser

Both my daughter and my daughter-in-law were expecting baby girls during the time that I was writing this book, so I could not resist this compressed wood organiser. I loved the cloud shape and the fact that it can be used for baby products, bibs, baby booties or anything else that needs to be at hand. I used glitter podge which shimmers beautifully when it catches the light.

1. Apply two coats of pink paint to the organiser. Make sure the first is dry before applying the second.

2. Use the dry brush technique (see page 21) to create wispy, feathery clouds over the pink paint to echo the cloud shape.

3. Carefully cut out the bear motifs and arrange them on the organiser.

4. Apply wood glue to the back of the motifs and affix them in place.

5. Use the brayer to smooth out any air bubbles.

6. Apply four layers of glitter podge in different directions (from top to bottom and from left to right) to the entire organiser. Allow each layer to dry completely before applying the next.

You'll need

Compressed wood organiser

Acrylic paint (Heritage: Baby Pink; white)

Brushes

Wrapping paper with bear motifs

Pair of scissors

Wood glue

Small brayer

Glitter podge

Bunting

These wooden flags are very durable and can be tailor made for several uses with a bit of paint and decoupage. I painted them pink for the nursery and then covered them with Decopatch paper. Apply the usual four layers of podge and allow to dry completely before turning over the flags and trimming any excess paper and opening up the holes. I used ribbon threaded through the holes to attach the flags, but cord will also do.

Window lace

Instead of a curtain for a bathroom window, lace can be podged to the glass. It not only looks pretty, it also ensures privacy. Using lace allows enough light into the bathroom. I tried both methods and found that it works better if the podge is applied over the lace rather than applying it to the window and then fixing the lace in place.

1. Measure the size of the window you want to cover. You will need that amount of lace, plus 2 cm (⁴/₅ in.) at the top and on the side (that is 1 cm (²/₅ in.) right around).

2. Use clothes-pegs or something similar to hold the lace in place at the top of the window pane so that it does not slip down while you are working.

3. Thoroughly saturate the lace with podge and use the brush to press it firmly onto the window pane. Work slowly, one section at a time, and be patient. Take care that the lace does not stretch.

4. Leave the podge to dry completely and use a craft knife to trim the excess lace up against the window frame.

You'll need

Lace (enough for the window you want to cover)

Pair of scissors

Podge – matt

Brush

Clothes-pegs

Craft knife

Small decorative tiles

Before

A problem often experienced in older houses is that the grout between the wall and the bath or washbasin comes loose and falls out, which is rather unsightly. This problem can be solved creatively by temporarily fixing smaller tiles in place over the grout. I podged scrapbook paper onto the tiles and used CPG to make them water resistant.

1. Cut the scrapbook paper into squares the same size as the tiles. This paper is sturdy and thick and cannot be folded over the edges of the tiles. If you use napkins or Decopatch paper, you can fold it neatly over the edges.

2. Use podge to stick the scrapbook paper to the tiles; work neatly and accurately. Leave the podge to dry.

3. Apply at least three layers of CPG podge to the tiles; make sure that the podge dries completely between layers.

4. Bake the tiles in a preheated oven at 90 °C (194 °F) for an hour.

5. Allow the tiles to cool completely. Use double-sided tape to stick them over the unsightly grout.

You'll need

5 cm (2 in.) square porcelain tiles (enough for the area that needs to be covered)

Scrapbook paper

Craft knife

Cutting mat

Podge – matt

Brush

CPG podge

Double-sided tape

Ladder towel-rack

New life was breathed into a rickety old ladder that was standing in our garage when one of my daughters suggested that I turn it into a towel rack. A pretty piece of scap fabric from the bargain bin of a textile shop was just the right size to decoupage the top step.

Before

1. Sand the ladder thoroughly to remove any unsightly stains and spots of paint. Wipe with a damp cloth to remove all the dust.

2. Apply a colourwash to the entire ladder (see page 21) and allow to dry completely.

3. Apply a layer of podge to the entire ladder to achieve a smooth finish and to protect the paint finish.

4. Cut the fabric to size to cover the top and sides of the top step.

5. Place the fabric over the step and use a liberal amount of podge to adhere it to the top step, saturating the fabric. Make neat folds at the corners and use enough podge to take the fabric over and around the sides. Allow to dry completely.

6. Use wood glue to adhere rubber strips to the bottom of the legs to ensure that the towel rack does not slip when positioned against the wall.

You'll need

Steps of an old ladder

220-grit sandpaper

Damp cloth

Chalk paint (I used white)

Brushes

Podge – matt

Fabric (big enough for the top step)

Pair of scissors

Rubber strips

Wood glue

Plastic table

The surface of this plastic kiddies' table was spoilt by ugly scratch marks, but the table itself was still sturdy and in a very good condition. I decided to give it a new lease of life with a decoupaged table top using fun, colourful napkins.

Before

1. Cut each napkin into quarters. Separate the layers and use only the top layer.

2. Apply spray adhesive to the coloured paper and carefully glue the napkins onto the paper. This makes it easy to work with the napkins.

3. Use the steel ruler and craft knife to cut out squares of 15 x 15 cm (6 x 6 in.). This is the size of a quarter of the napkin.

4. Arrange the napkins close to one another on the table top. They will cover the table top but leave a 1,5 cm (³/₅ in.) border right around. Mark this border lightly in pencil.

5. Apply podge to approximately half of the table top and carefully press each napkin square in place. Use the brayer to smooth out any air bubbles. Repeat the process with the other half of the table.

6. Adhere a strip of Washi tape in the open border right around the napkin squares to round off the table top.

7. Apply four layers of podge in different directions (from top to bottom and from left to right) over the whole table top. Allow each layer to dry completely before applying the next.

8. Lastly, apply a coat of heavy duty high gloss varnish.

You'll need

Hard plastic table

4 brightly coloured napkins with matching motifs

Pair of scissors

16 A4 sheets of coloured paper in 4 different colours

Spray adhesive

Craft knife

Cutting mat

Steel ruler

Pencil

Podge – outdoor

Brushes

Small brayer

Washi tape

Heavy duty high gloss varnish

Wall niche

Many houses built in a certain era have wall niches on inside or outside walls, which can be used for display purposes. This niche at the front door of the house was decorated in subtle shades using napkins with rose and butterfly motifs. The decoupage was finished with natural rope that fitted in nicely with the whorled-rope effect of the plaster-work.

Before

1. Wash the niche with soapy water and allow to dry.

2. Cut the napkins into different shapes and sizes, keeping the motifs whole. Separate the layers of the napkin and use only the top layer.

3. First plan your composition and then use podge to apply the napkin pieces to the wall. The pieces can overlap because they are so thin. I tried to place the bigger motifs such as the roses where they are clearly visible and used butterflies and birds to fill the gaps in-between.

4. Once the whole surface has been covered with the napkins, apply four layers of podge to the entire area in different directions (from top to bottom and from left to right). Allow each layer to dry completely before applying the next.

5. Use wood glue to adhere the twine along the edge of the niche. You will have to be patient when you get to the top of the curve because the glue does not dry immediately and you need to hold it in position. Apply a layer of varnish to the niche and the twine once the glue has dried completely.

You'll need

3 napkins

Podge for outdoor use

Heavy duty high gloss varnish

Brushes

Wood glue

Enough twine to go right around the niche

Planters

Gardening in pots is much easier than in flower beds; this is why I really love pots of different shapes and sizes. Rough cement pots are much cheaper than ceramic or porcelain pots. The contemporary designs on the Decopatch paper and the high gloss varnish finish make these pots look like the real McCoy. To achieve a smooth effect, the surface of the pot must be treated with jointing plaster or a similar product.

Before

1. Sand the cement pots with the 80-grit sandpaper to obtain the smoothest possible effect.

2. Use a pallet knife to apply the jointing plaster to the pots as evenly as possible and allow to dry completely before sanding the pots with the 220-grit sandpaper.

3. Repeat step 2 until the pots are smooth enough to your liking and paint the pots with the white PVA paint. My husband, Paul, repeated this step four times before he applied the paint!

4. Carefully plan how you are going to put the Decopatch paper on the pots. A sheet of paper is only 30 x 40 cm (11¾ x 15¾ in.), so you will have to join the sheets. Fortunately, this paper works well on curves and because it is so thin, you cannot see the joins at all.

5. Cover the pots with whole sheets of paper where possible. If it is necessary to join the paper at the corners of the pot, first place pieces of paper over the corner and then paste whole sheets over them. This makes the joins disappear.

6. Apply four layers of podge to the pots in different directions (from top to bottom and from left to right). Allow each layer to dry completely before applying the next.

7. Finish the pots with a coat of high gloss varnish.

You'll need

Three pots in different sizes

80- and 220-grit sandpaper

Jointing plaster (used on ceilings)

Pallet knife

White PVA paint

Brushes

10 sheets of Decopatch paper in shades of black and white (the amount will depend on the size of the pots)

Podge – outdoor

Heavy duty high gloss varnish

Mini chest of drawers

Before

It was very difficult for me to choose between two mini chests of drawers (also see page 124) at my favourite craft shop and because I had stacks of beautiful Decopatch paper, I was obliged to buy both. This chest with its two rows of drawers of different depths is very versatile. I use it to store my calligraphy supplies. The old-fashioned rose and cursive writing pattern of the paper complement each other and conjure up an image of an old writing-table with an inkpot and quill on it.

You'll need

Compressed wood mini chest of drawers

Acrylic paint (Heritage: Coral Pink)

Brushes

Decopatch paper (I used roses and cursive writing)

Pair of scissors

Podge – satin

Small brayer

Craft knife

1. Apply two coats of coral pink paint to the frame and the front and sides of the drawers. Allow the first coat to dry completely before applying the second.

2. Cut the Decopatch paper into strips that are big enough to cover the front of each drawer and fold over the sides and top edge.

3. Apply podge to the front of each drawer, paste the right size paper strip onto it and use the brayer to smooth out any air bubbles. Neatly fold the paper around the corners. With Decopatch paper this is easily done.

4. Allow to dry, then use a craft knife to neatly trim the paper around the opening in the upper edge of each drawer.

5. Apply four layers of podge in different directions (from left to right and from top to bottom) to the front of each drawer. Allow to dry thoroughly between layers.

6. Apply one layer of podge to all the painted sections to protect the paint.

Document chest

Before

This sturdy wooden chest is reminiscent of my childhood. My father kept important documents such as birth certificates, registration papers, graduation certificates, etcetera, in it. One of his colleagues made the chest out of hard pine. This is one of the items that I 'harvested' from my parents' garage for the book.

1.   Remove the chest handle, hinges and clasps so that the lid and rest of the chest are separated and easy to work with.

2.   Lightly sand the outside with 200-grit sandpaper. One of the advantages of decoupage, is that you do not have to do as much preparation than if you were painting the case.

3.   Cut the scrapbook paper into rectangles and squares of different sizes and arrange them on the suitcase to determine where you are going to paste them.

4.   Apply wood glue to the reverse side of the rectangles and squares and cover the suitcase with them. Do not allow the paper to overlap – it is thick and makes unsightly ridges. Use the brayer to smooth out any air bubbles and allow the glue to dry completely.

5.   Sand the edges and corners of the suitcase with 200-grit paper to create a weathered look.

6.   Apply four layers of podge in different directions (from top to bottom and from left to right) to the whole chest. Allow each layer to dry completely before applying the next.

7.   Sand the case with 1000-grit sandpaper until it is completely dull and smooth.

8.   Apply four more layers of podge as before and screw the hinges, handle and clasps back in place.

You'll need

Wooden chest

Screwdriver

200- and 1000-grit sandpaper

Scrapbook paper with vintage theme

Pair of scissors

Wood glue

Brush

Small brayer

Podge – matt

Brushes

Suitcase for stamps

Before

My husband is an avid stamp collector and when I came across this handy little wooden case, I immediately decided to decorate it with decoupage so that he could use it for the stamps he was sorting. The crackle varnish worked particularly well on the scrapbook paper with an envelope and postcard theme, which perfectly suited the purpose of the case. You can finish the inside of the case with paint and a layer of felt.

You'll need

Compressed wood case

Screwdriver

Scrapbook paper

Pair of scissors

Brushes

Wood glue

Small brayer

Podge – matt

Crackle varnish (Heritage: Antique Crackle base and top coat for big cracks)

Dark brown wax

Soft cloth

1. Remove the case handle, hinges and clasps so that the lid and rest of the case are separated and easy to work with.

2. Cut the scrapbook paper into rectangles and squares of different sizes and arrange them on the case to determine where you are going to paste them.

3. Apply wood glue to the reverse side of the rectangles and squares and cover the outer surfaces of the case with them. Use the brayer to smooth out any air bubbles and allow the glue to dry completely.

4. Apply two layers of podge in different directions over the whole case. Allow each layer to dry completely before applying the next.

5. Apply a base coat of crackle varnish to the entire case. Allow it to dry and apply a second layer in the opposite direction.

6. As soon as the base layer is completely dry, apply the crackle topcoat (just one layer). The cracks form while the topcoat dries.

7. Use a soft cloth to cover the case in dark brown wax. The wax will be absorbed into the cracks and create an antique look. Polish the case until it has a soft shine.

8. Replace the clasps, hinges and handle.

Sewing room chest of drawers

Before

Library card catalogue drawers are ideal for a sewing room because they offer an orderly storage space for various small needlework items such as cotton, bobbins, pins, needles, measuring tapes, buttons, hooks and eyes and other fasteners. Nowadays most libraries store all their information on computers, so these drawers have become obsolete as far as their original purpose is concerned. Do yourself a favour and find one. I have seen a number for sale on e-bay.

You'll need

Library card catalogue chest of drawers

Screwdriver

Chalk paint (Heritage: Sea Shepard, Annie Sloan: Province and Emile – choose paint that will suit the colour of your paper)

Brushes

Masking tape

Scrapbook paper with a needlework theme

Podge – satin

Pair of scissors

Small brayer

1. Remove all the brass pulls and paint the whole chest in blue except the frames around the drawers. Apply two coats and allow the first to dry completely before applying the second.

2. Stick masking tape around the front frame and apply two coats of turquoise paint to the frame. Allow the first coat to dry completely before applying the second.

3. Apply two layers of satin podge to the paint to prevent it from being damaged or scratched off.

4. Apply two coats of purple chalk paint to the front of the drawers. Allow the first coat to dry completely before applying the second.

5. Cut the scrapbook paper slightly smaller than the flat front section of the drawers.

6. Use podge to paste the paper onto the drawers and use the brayer to smooth out any air bubbles.

7. Apply four layers of podge in different directions (from top to bottom and from left to right) to the front of the drawers (including the painted edges). Allow each layer to dry completely before applying the next.

8. Replace the brass pulls.

Chest of drawers for colouring station

Before

The colouring bug really bit me and I have a collection of colouring pencils – oil based, water based, metal finish, watercolour, gel pens, koki pens, sharpeners, erasers second to none. You name it, I have it! This mini chest of drawers is ideal for storing everything together and I can move it to wherever I am working. It can be used to store any craft items.

You'll need

- Compressed wood mini chest of drawers
- Acrylic paint (Heritage: Storm Grey)
- Brushes
- Decopatch paper (I used different patterns in matching colours)
- Pair of scissors
- Podge – satin
- Craft knife
- Cutting mat

1. Apply two coats of grey paint to the frame and the front and sides of the drawers. Allow the first coat to dry completely before applying the second.

2. Cut a selection of Decopatch papers into squares and rectangles.

3. Apply podge to the front of each drawer and paste pieces of paper on them randomly but in an orderly fashion. Use your fingers to smooth out any air bubbles because the pieces of paper are so small.

4. Allow to dry. Place each drawer, with the front facing downwards, on the cutting mat and neatly trim any excess paper.

5. Apply four layers of podge in different directions (from left to right and from top to bottom) to the front of each drawer. Allow to dry thoroughly between layers.

6. Apply one layer of podge to the entire chest to protect the paint.

Notice board

Although we live in a technological age where most of our appointments are stored on cell phones and in electronic diaries, a notice board like this one is functional and also looks good. It is also a good place to keep items that are easily misplaced in the study such as keys, a pair of scissors and a measuring tape. The framed metal sheet with magnets helps you keep an eye on important information.

1. Decorate the wood canvas using the cracked paint technique (see page 23) and allow to dry completely.

2. Paint the paper roll holder, the flat wooden frame and the scissors holder in the light colour acrylic paint. Apply more than one coat if necessary.

3. Cut out the book motifs, apply podge to the reverse side and carefully fix in place on the wood approximately 5 cm (2 in.) from the bottom edge. Use the brayer to smooth out any air bubbles.

4. Apply two layers of podge in different directions over the paper only. Make sure that the first layer is completely dry before applying the second. Apply a third layer to the entire board.

5. Using wood glue, cover the metal sheet with the scrapbook paper and affix the wooden frame to the sheet.

6. Use the drawing-pins and thick rubber band to attach the paper roll to the paper roll holder.

7. Screw the metal strip to the bottom of the paper roll holder where the paper will be torn off.

8. Use the screws to attach the paper roll holder and the scissors holder to the wood canvas and screw the hooks in place.

9. Use wood glue to affix the framed metal plate to the wood canvas. Place a few heavy books on top while the glue dries to ensure that it is firmly stuck in place.

You'll need

Wood canvas of 62 x 75 x 4 cm (25 x 30 x 1½ in.)

Acrylic paint (Heritage: Oatmeal and Chocolate)

Brushes

Kwik crack

Sponge applicator

Scissors holder blank

Paper roll holder blank

Flat wooden frame 20 x 25 cm (8 x 10 in.)

Paper with book motifs (I used wallpaper)

Pair of scissors

Podge – matt

Small brayer

Metal sheet 18 x 23 cm (7 x 9 in.) and scrapbook paper to cover it

Wood glue

2 drawing-pins and thick rubber band for paper roll

Metal strip for paper roll holder

Screws

3 screw-in hooks

Letter and document holders

This document holder made of compressed wood is slightly bigger than an A4 size paper and is ideal to have on your desk to house documents that need your attention. The wooden holder was painted on the inside with Heritage: Olivia chalk paint and the outside was decoupaged with world-map paper. I also applied a layer of podge to the paint on the inside to prevent it being damaged or scratched.

The letter holder was also painted with Olivia, the outside decoupaged with world-map paper and the paint covered with one layer of podge to protect it. The decoupaged sections of both the document holder and letter holder were covered in four layers of podge applied in different directions over the paper.